My Sister's Keeper

Kerry Duke, Editor

Publishing Designs, Inc.
Huntsville, Alabama

Publishing Designs, Inc.
P. O. Box 3241
Huntsville, Alabama

Second Printing, 2001

Library of Congress Cataloging-in-Publication Data

My sister's keeper / Kerry Duke, editor.
     p. cm.
  Includes bibliographical references.
  ISBN 0-929540-23-9 (pbk.)
  1. Women--Religious life. 2. Christian ethics. 3. Christian life. I. Duke,
Kerry, 1959-

BV4527 .M9 1999
248.8'43--dc21

                                 99-052032

Printed in the United States of America

CONTENTS

Part Four: Current Issues

Part Five: Special Areas

Acknowledgments

The Christian women who wrote this book bring a wealth of experience and knowledge to its pages. They have taken time from already busy schedules in order to complete this book. Each one of them is well qualified for the subjects she addresses. Each one has a special way of writing. Each one speaks from the heart as well as from the Scriptures. If this book enjoys the circulation we pray it will, their work for this book will benefit many. Their words will be appreciated in various places by Christian women, perhaps many of whom will never personally meet these writers. These authors have rendered a great service to Christian women. I commend them for the excellent job they have done in this book.

Ideas for the contents of this book came from many Christian women. Their help has been very valuable. The original idea for the book itself, however, came from one person. One of my duties at Tennessee Bible College is to oversee library personnel. One of our workers at the time, Tamyra Templeton, suggested that I compile and edit a book for women's studies written by various Christian women. Her suggestion was given immediate approval and support from other women. Had she not mentioned this idea to me, this book would not have been written.

Introduction

Women enjoy and need good books. Christian women, both as groups and as individuals, treasure writings that help them in their Christian walk. Excellent books have been written for general audiences of men and women, benefiting greatly their readers. But sometimes women crave a book with a special sensitivity to their needs, to their unique situation. They need to know that the writer understands their feelings and sympathizes with their problems. Ideally, they need a book written by Christian women to Christian women.

This book is practical. It deals with real needs, real problems, and real situations commonly experienced by women. The writers address these questions from a woman's viewpoint, giving direction and encouragement from the Scriptures and offering counsel based on years of experience. They do not avoid difficult questions or painful issues. When they speak about these situations, they often do so from personal experience. They do not offer shallow, simplistic answers to serious and complex problems. They do not suggest quick and easy remedies for situations that require major surgery. Instead, they lend a sympathetic ear to the situations and then firmly explain relevant Bible teaching.

While this book is a practical one, it is not merely driven by an aim to be practical. The trend in this generation is for easy reading, and books with a practical thrust fit this trend well. Sales in the book market generally confirm this trend. The television age has left many with little desire for reading, and if they do read, they want books that entertain rather than challenge. So the temptation for writers is to accommodate this demand with hollow platitudes rather than substance. When the writing is on a spiritual theme, the result is a book that reads like a transcript of a television talk show and scarcely discusses God's Word. These books, of course, often sell well because they are entertaining and because readers from a wide variety of conflicting religious beliefs feel safe in reading them. Meanwhile, questions of right and wrong, issues concerning heaven and hell, and distinctions between true and false doctrine go untouched.

Questions regarding Bible interpretation and false doctrine are not interesting to some, but they should be. And though such questions are rarely discussed in books for women, this book deals with such issues for just that reason. In fact, the primary reason for producing this book is the need for such material, as well as material that is considered practical. As a result, this book addresses false teaching on the role of women in the church as well as the need for a fervent prayer life. It deals with divorce and remarriage as well as kindness in the home. It confronts issues like abortion and indecent dress as well as the discipline of children in the home. This unique balance is one of the strengths of this work.

Christian women of all kinds will enjoy this book: wives, singles, mothers, widows, preachers' wives, and other Christian women. We are excited to release it to the public. Its pages will, God willing, help many women to be strong in the Lord—women after God's own heart.

Kerry Duke
October 1999

PART ONE

You

1

Time for Self
Irene C. Taylor

Introduction

That there is need for some quality personal time for self will not be denied. We live in a stress-filled world. Life on the "fast track" produces its own set of problems, one of which is a lack of time for proper attention to the needs of self.

Jesus recognized the need for personal, private time on occasion. Often He felt the need to remove Himself from the throng for a few precious moments of quiet time (Matt. 14:23; Mark 6:46; John 6:15). Prior to His betrayal at the hands of Judas Iscariot, He separated Himself from the Inner Three and prayed alone to the Father above (Matt. 26:39, 42, 44). There is no better one to whom to turn in time of stress than the heavenly Father.

Today's woman has a multifaceted role to fill, perhaps more than in any previous generation. This is in part due to the influence of the Feminist Movement. Although our mothers and grandmothers had more hard manual labor to do than do we, their role was primarily that of wife, mother, and grandmother. Many of them helped with labor on the farm but few worked in public work outside the home turf. Those who did returned home to stay after the workday. Today Superwoman tries to be Susie Professional in addition to participating in many prestigious civic and community endeavors. If she is married and has a family, she must somehow sandwich in basic responsibilities in the home. There is no way she can do a completely adequate job in any area and frustration is a sure byproduct. We women often are slow to accept the fact that we cannot do it all and maintain our personal balance. We may feel guilty when we cannot.

Everyone is entitled to a few quiet moments to clear those cobwebs from the mind. "Be still and know that I am God" (Ps. 46:10). There is an old saying which suggests that we take time to "stop and smell the roses." What sage advice that really is. A period of diversion can do wonders to grant a new perspective to life. The roses of life will not bloom forever. We must enjoy them while we can.

What are we really here for? We would do well to stop and ask ourselves this important question frequently. If we would reflect on our real purpose in life, perhaps we could avoid overloading ourselves in that needless quest for things. Much of what we expend our energy to acquire is unnecessary. Likely, we would be better off without some of it. In our rush to acquire a certain status of life we lose sight of the fact that we are here for such a short time to prepare for eternity.

Time for self must be kept in its proper perspective. We must avoid the temptation to become absorbed in self to the point of selfishness. It is wrong to live for the "I" to the exclusion of a proper consideration for others. It is not wrong to set aside a *reasonable* time to renew one's mind, body, and soul. One should never feel guilty for so doing. It promotes spiritual, mental, emotional, and physical good health. This helps us grow "in wisdom and stature, and in favor with God and man" (Luke 2:52). The trick is to find that special time on a regular basis. This is especially true for young mothers but it is true for any family woman. Family needs cannot be scheduled. Take heart in the fact that this problem is not unique to woman; man faces the issue as well.

While setting aside a time for self, several areas must be given consideration. While our primary interests are for God and family—and in that order—our emotional state is due for its fair share. "Happiness is inward and not outward; and so it does not depend on what we have, but on what we are" (Henry Van Dyke). Pursuing a special interest to divert the mind from daily stress is wise. It may be a hobby that one finds enjoyable, one as simple as reading a *good* book. It may be visiting the sick and shut-ins. It may be gardening or taking a walk in the fresh air, truly "smelling the roses." This part of self-time may not be available daily. However, one should make an earnest effort to schedule periodic times just to enjoy life whether alone or with one's treasured companion.

Though considered strange by the masses, many Christians find real enjoyment in the "diversion" of travel to religious gatherings such as, for example, sound lectureships and gospel meetings. These times serve a twofold purpose: they strengthen one's faith and bring one into a closer, more precious relationship with God. They can have the added benefit of building a closer relationship with fellow Christians and broadening one's circle of friends. Whatever one's choice, there is a need for attention to self. It goes without saying that one's choice should be uplifting and in harmony with the Christian life.

How can one live in peace and harmony with others when he is constantly at odds with self? We are admonished, "If it be possible, as much as lieth in you, live peaceably with all men" (Rom. 12:18). Much has been said in recent years about self-esteem. While this writer feels the concept of self-esteem has been overdone, the right kind is a necessary ingredient to the well-rounded personality. It just needs to be maintained in proper perspective. Self is not the sum total of life.

While a study of this nature cannot pursue in detail every aspect of the need for self, a few of the vital areas will be given consideration.

Time for Personal Bible Study

"Study to shew *thyself* approved unto God, a workman that needeth not to be ashamed, rightly dividing the word of truth" (2 Tim. 2:15, emphasis added). Note the personal tone of that command (and it is a command). No one can study for you or me but we ourselves. I have often commented that if one could become knowledgeable by association (like guilt by association) I could be a much wiser woman! But my husband's vast knowledge cannot transfer to me by osmosis. We each must achieve our own storehouse of knowledge. And no person is wise who knows only the wisdom of the world. Biblical knowledge is of far more importance. Again, inspiration has Paul to write, "And that *ye* study to be quiet, and to do *your* own business, and to work with *your* own hands, as we commanded *you*" (1 Thess. 4:11, emphasis supplied). Again, we note the personal tone of the command. "O how love *I* the law! it is *my* meditation all the day" (Ps. 119:97, emphasis supplied).

There is no substitute for regular, personal Bible study. In our whirlwind lifestyle, it is often hard to set aside a special study time for learning more of God's Word. There are those who find the early morning hours more conducive to this goal. They arise early before family activities begin. My husband has followed this schedule successfully for years. Others, like myself, find it difficult to concentrate early in the day. A later hour proves a better choice for these. The secret to real success, sometimes hard to achieve, is to do it regularly. Unexpected and unscheduled events more easily interfere with the time set aside later in the day, yet determination can usually overcome such upsets.

It is helpful to have a plan of study outlined. Various plans have been devised and the student is free to choose the one most suited to her. Some plans schedule specific passages for each day; others use a topical approach, concentrating on a given subject for a given time. My husband

and I have chosen to read through the whole Bible each year with a slight variation in our individual approach. By reading carefully three chapters each day in both the Old and New Testaments, one can easily cover the entire Bible. This will take one through the Old Testament once and the New Testament four times during the year. It is amazing how much clearer the New Testament becomes by becoming more familiar with the Old Testament.

The Bible has much to say about the proper attitude toward God's Word. The psalmist says it well: "Thy word is a lamp unto my feet, and a light unto my path . . . Thy testimonies have I taken as an heritage for ever: for they are the rejoicing of my heart" (Ps. 119:105-111). A wise parent wrote on the flyleaf of his son's Bible: "This book will keep you from sin. Sin will keep you from this book." The wise man of Proverbs declares: "For the commandment is a lamp, and the law is light; and reproofs of instruction are the way of life" (Prov. 6:23).

The strength gained from allowing more of God's word into our hearts (minds) will pay great dividends. In the instruction to wives, Peter admonishes us to concentrate more on the inner being than on our outward appearance.

> Whose adorning let it not be that outward adorning of plaiting the hair, and of wearing of gold, or of putting on of apparel: but let it be the hidden man of the heart, in that which is not corruptible, even the ornament of a meek and quiet spirit, which is in the sight of God of great price (1 Pet. 3:3-4).

It is the "ornament of a meek and quiet spirit" with which we adorn ourselves. To acquire this spirit, this inner peace so priceless, make a regular date for a visit with God.

In addition to our private, personal Bible study we must make a regular practice of attending public worship assemblies of our home congregation. The association and fellowship in worship with our fellow Christians give strength gained in no other way. This is a valuable gift to self. The words of a beautiful song seem appropriate here.

Time For Prayer

The world has lost the right of prayer,
And saints have failed to pray;
What loss sustained beyond repair!
How blind of heart are they!

The Father speaketh in His word,
He talks no other way!
But to converse with Him, our Lord,
We must take time to pray!

There is no trial, grief or pain,
No moment of the day,
But that we may in Jesus' name
Incline our souls and pray!

Chorus:

Pray in the Morning,
Pray at the Noontime,
Pray in the Evening
Pray all the time.

Pray when you're happy,
Pray when in sorrow,
Pray when you're tempted,
Pray all the time![1]

There is power and strength in prayer. Truly, the hour of prayer is sweet. Regular prayer should be a part of the Christian's life—daily. Our friendship with God should be a two-way relationship. He talks to us through His Word; we talk to Him in prayer. Most of us quickly turn to Him in prayer when trouble comes. We need to pray in good times as well. As one gentleman expressed, "I want to pray often so that God knows who I am." We need God all the time.

[1] Sanderson, L. O., Editor, *Christian Hymns III*, (Nashville, Tennessee: Gospel Advocate Company, 1966), p. 289.

There is a definite design to acceptable prayer. It is to be addressed to God the Father. Jesus, our perfect example, always addressed petitions to the Father, never to Himself or the Holy Spirit (Matt. 6:9; 11:25; 26:39, 42; John 17:1). We are to address Him reverently. We are instructed to express our thankfulness to God for the bountiful blessings He bestows (James 1:17). We are to thank Him for the gift of His Son (2 Cor. 9:15). We and are to pray for our daily needs and for forgiveness of our sins (Matt. 6:11, 14-15). We are to ask our petition in Jesus' name (John 14:13; 15:16; 16:23). We are to be mindful of the needs of others (James 5:16). We are to pray for our elders and for rulers of the nations (Acts 20:36; 1 Tim. 2:1-2; Heb. 13:7). We certainly are to pray for our loved ones, for the sick and bereaved, and for those who need our encouragement in any way. We are also to pray for our enemies (Matt. 5:44). It is difficult to retain feelings of animosity toward one for whom we sincerely pray.

Prayer is an avenue whereby we may release the stress of life. It is, therefore, of great benefit to our "self" well-being. When we leave our problems in God's hands we find renewed courage to face what lies ahead. Though God knows our needs before we ask, we need the humbling experience of knowing we are dependent on Him. For our own good, we need to make time for private prayer.

Time for Good Health Habits

Common sense tells us that it is a mark of wisdom to observe good health rules. We have a dual obligation to take care of our bodies and keep them pure.

> And God hath both raised up the Lord, and will also raise up us by his own power. Know ye not that your bodies are the members of Christ? Shall I then take the members of Christ, and make them the members of an harlot? God forbid. What? Know ye not that he which is joined to an harlot is one body? For two, saith he, shall be one flesh. But he that is joined unto the Lord is one spirit. Flee fornication.

Every sin that a man doeth is without the body; but he that committeth fornication sinneth against his own body. What? Know ye not that your body is the temple of the Holy Ghost, which is in you, which ye have of God, and ye are not your own? For ye are bought with a price: therefore glorify God in your body, and in your spirit, which are God's (1 Cor. 6:14-20).

If we really understood the truth of this passage, we would exercise greater care in practicing good health habits.

Perhaps we need to give serious reflection on God's view of our careless lifestyle. It seems apparent that God is not pleased when we engage in habits and abuses harmful to the body. Though some do not agree, it seems logical to this writer from these verses that God does not approve of such harmful indulgences as alcohol, addictive drugs, tobacco use in any form, or gambling in any form. The practice of illegitimate free love and perverted sexual practices have resulted in fatal sexual diseases. Surely God abhors these practices (Rom. 1:24ff; 1 Cor. 6:9ff). Even closer home, foolish are we when we ignore sensible eating habits and indulge freely in foods known to be harmful or in quantities injurious to our well-being.

Exercise of the proper kind is a contribution toward good health. Here again, exercise must be kept in perspective. Paul writes, "For bodily exercise profiteth little: but godliness is profitable unto all things" (1 Tim. 4:8). Inspiration recognized that exercise has a place in our lives but it is not to be the main thrust. In comparison to our quest for godliness, exercise profiteth little. The insatiable thirst for pleasure and fun by many today overlooks the real purpose of life. In judgment it will be our godly life which will matter, not the proficiency of our exercise. Exercise is profitable inasmuch as it enhances our health and enables us to serve Him better.

When engaging in exercise the Christian will give heed to the law of modesty in apparel. Many forms of exercise are in and of themselves good, but the attire worn is suspect. *Such attire is not necessary; we have only allowed ourselves to believe that it is!* For years Christians *knew* what constituted modest apparel. Then Satan succeeded in convincing many that it is just too hot to go fully dressed! Today it is hard to distinguish many in the church from those of the world. It is of personal concern that elders, deacons, preachers, and Bible teachers are among the guilty. There is no separate set of rules for these except that they are in an added position of influence. How can the preacher teach regarding modest apparel when his is as brief as that of the world? How can elders admonish the congregation when they and their families participate? The answer has been that, rather than give up their own immodesty, they remain silent in opposition to such. Part of taking care of self is taking the time to understand and observe God's law for proper appearance in public. We should have enough self-pride and self-interest to want to be governed by His rules of modest attire.

Good health requires adequate sleep. Except under special circumstances every effort should be made to get adequate sleep. We may be able to get by on three to five hours of sleep for a while, but sooner or later it will catch up with us and affect our good health. Remember, we are God's temple. He deserves that we observe good maintenance and upkeep as much as is humanly possible.

Good health requires good medical attention when needed. While no one advocates unnecessary doctor visits for every ache or pain, it is poor maintenance of God's temple to ignore a real medical need. Granted, there are those who rush to the doctor for every little matter demanding a pill as a cure. Then there are those who seemingly refuse help when it is really needed. Neither stance is conducive to taking care of self. And let it be noted here that medical help is sometimes needed for emotional problems. Due to many causes, many of which are beyond our control, special help is needed. No one would fault the person who seeks medical attention for a broken limb or a heart problem. Why, then, do we fault those who battle with depression and related problems? We display our ignorance and lack of compassion when we rashly attribute such to weakness of faith! It is no more a disgrace to suffer from and seek medical assistance for the latter than it is to solicit help for the former. The latter often results from changes in the body's chemistry. Let us be more compassionate toward those facing such problems. Let us be careful to take the time to obtain the necessary medical attention for self no matter what the need.

Time For Friendship

How empty life would be without friends! The wise man of Proverbs gives the formula for making friends. "A man that hath [maketh, ASV] friends must show himself friendly" (Prov. 18:24). Friendship is a two-way avenue. No matter how gracious and friendly one party may be, he/she cannot mold a friendship alone. When we find ourselves alone, especially in times of trials, we need to look deep inside for the reason. How many times have *I* "been there" for someone else in difficult times? How often have *I* taken a meal to a family facing sickness and trouble? How often have *I* offered to sit with the sick so the caregiver might have a few moments of relief? To *have* a friend we must *be* a friend. The story is told of the couple considering a new town. While inquiring about the people of the town they turned to an elderly gentleman for an honest appraisal. He asked how the people were in the town they were leaving. Upon being told that they were very unfriendly, the gentleman replied that that was how the people in this town were. Soon after, another couple made the same inquiry. They reported the people in the town they left were friendly and kind. The gentleman reported the people in this town were the same. Why did he answer thus? Because we find about what we look for! If we want to have friends, we have to make ourselves friend-worthy.

Friendship calls for an investment of time. "A friend loveth at all times, and a brother is born for adversity" (Prov. 17:17). "A friend is one who comes to you when all others leave."[2] When hard times come, our real friends stay to help us through. Everyone needs true friends. Many beautiful tributes have been written about friendship. Reflect on just a few shared below.

- A friend is a present you give yourself.

- A friend is one who knows all about you and still loves you.

- A friend is a person with whom you dare to be yourself.

- The light of friendship is like the light of phosphorus, sun when all around is dark.

- Friendship is the only cement that will ever hold the world together.

- Friendship is to be purchased only by friendship.[3]

As a gift to yourself, make time for friends. It is so easy to allow one's time to become so filled that little time is left to share the joy of friendship. We cheat ourselves greatly when we permit this to occur. Make time to share a cup of coffee; share a lunch or an afternoon visit. Sharing the love which flows between true friends is a gift indescribable. Rich is the person who has a true friend regardless of his financial status. Poor indeed is the one who lacks a true friend though he may have amassed great wealth.

Friendship is essential to the well-being of a whole person. Fortunate indeed is that one whose best friend on earth is her companion! Life is made sweeter when husband, friend, lover, and father of one's children comes wrapped

[2] Petty, Jo, *Apples of Gold*, (Norwalk, Connecticut: C. R. Gibson Company), p. 17.
[3] Ibid., pp. 15, 14, 13, 11, 15, 10.

up in one treasured package. Forgotten is the author of
the verse below but cherished is the truth therein.

> Make new friends,
> But keep the old.
> The one is silver,
> The other gold.

True friendship helps one to grow. The wise man of Proverbs declares, "Faithful are the wounds of a friend" (Prov.
27:6). Only a real friend has the courage and caring to tell
us in love when we are wrong. We need that kind of love to
help us on life's rugged road.

Time to Reflect on Life's Goal

Every person must make a choice as to his/her destiny
for eternity. Two options are open to us: the broad way
whose destiny is destruction or the narrow way which leads
to life eternal (Matt. 7:13-14). This is the most important
decision one makes in life and it calls for time and wisdom.
This is a choice for self; no one can make it for us. The
cares of this life can so easily choke out the best of intentions. This is the lesson taught in the parable of the sower
(Matt. 13:18ff). Our dedication to regular Bible study will
greatly enhance our ability to keep focused on our goal.
From time to time we each would do well to stop and take
inventory of our life. Some soul-searching questions are in
order.

1. What is the most important thing in my life?
2. Do I really believe Matthew 6:33?
3. If I had to choose right now between a church activity
   and a secular one (such as a school, civic, or sports
   event) which would I choose?
4. With what do I fill my free time?
5. Do I *enjoy* Christian worship?
6. Do I enjoy Christian friendships or do I prefer association with the world?

7. Am I careful to remember that it matters how I conduct myself before others?
8. Do I believe it matters how I dress?
9. Do I do good works in the name of the church to God's glory?
10. Do I really live as though I want to go to heaven?

There is a peace and security in being a child of God that the world can never know (John 14:27). That peace comes only from knowing that one is in a right relationship with God. This relationship begins when we are obedient to God's will initially. This is accomplished by hearing God's Word (Rom. 10:17), believing that Word (Mark 16:16), repenting of one's sins (Luke 13:3), confessing Jesus as the Son of God (Rom. 10:9-10), and being buried in baptism (Rom. 6:4; 1 Pet. 3:21). Then the living of the Christian life brings a peace that surpasses all understanding (Phil. 4:7).

The words of the beautiful song sum up the reason for keeping our eyes and hearts turned toward heaven: "Heaven Will Surely Be Worth It All."

Neglect not to focus daily upon the promise of God. To those who faithfully serve Him all the days of their life, God has promised a reward in eternity. Take time to focus on heaven's glory. "And hereby we do *know* that we know him, if we keep his commandments" (1 John 2:3, emphasis supplied).

Conclusion

There is much wisdom in reserving a reasonable time for self. Physical exhaustion can be avoided by taking a much-needed break from regular activities. Emotional stress is relieved by a brief diversion.

Today's fast pace finds us pulled in so many directions that we scarcely know which way to turn first. Each of us needs to learn how to keep proper order of priority. Most of us have learned how to choose between good and bad. It becomes more difficult to choose between good, better, and best, between what is really necessary and what is not. Like the scribes, Pharisees, and hypocrites to whom Jesus spoke in Matthew 23:23, there are major things we ought to do without leaving minor things undone. Take time to learn the difference.

Again let it be emphasized that time for self be kept in balance. We must not neglect self for this can lead to a myriad of problems both spiritual and physical. The other side of the coin is that in recent times an overemphasis has been placed on self. Thus some today seem unable to look past what *I* want. The successful formula for real joy in life cannot be improved: J-esus first; 0-thers second; Y-ourself last. This in no sense need lead to neglect of self. Rather it emphasizes the order or priority which Jesus meant for the Christian to observe. Christianity is not to be a life of service to self; it is to be a life of service—period. That service should go to God first then to our fellow man, thus making our world a better place in which to live.

Time For Me

Each day I live upon this earth
Let me ever mindful be
That if I do my best for Thee,
I must take time for me.

May I never succumb to habits
That will harm and hurt my health.
A body strong; a pure, clean mind
Is better far than wealth.

Let me be mindful, Lord, of others
While focusing on Thee,
And know when all is said and done,
There will be time for *me*.

Irene C. Taylor
February 26, 1998

2

Why?

Jane McWhorter

Being a child of God has never implied an assurance that we would be free of difficulties. Troubles are going to come to all of us. In fact, they have been promised: "Man that is born of woman is of few days, and full of trouble" (Job 14:1). "In the world ye shall have tribulation: but be of good cheer; I have overcome the world" (John 16:33). "Yea, and all that live godly in Christ Jesus shall suffer persecution" (2 Tim. 3:12).

At one time or another, most of us have felt the anguish of Gideon when he questioned: "If the Lord be with us, why then is all this befallen us" (Judg. 6:13)? Suspended between heaven and earth, Christ Himself cried out: "My God, my God, why hast thou forsaken me" (Matt. 27:46)?

It is not wrong to question. To an honest heart that is searching for an answer, questioning can be a powerful exercise in strengthening the soul. The key lies in our attitude. Do we look at God *through* our hardships or do we look at hardships through *God?* Instead of asking *why* troubles come to God-fearing people, we should instead desire to learn what should happen to Christians *when* hardships strike.

Just as Christian wives may be instrumental in winning their unbelieving husbands to Christ by their manner of life if the husband will not listen to the Word of God (1 Pet. 3:1-2), so can Christians teach powerful lessons to the world by the way they handle adversities.

Some lessons are forged on the anvil of life, and their meanings are not soon forgotten. The seeds of this study were planted in my mind a number of years ago when my mother was stricken with a painful and deforming malady, rheumatoid arthritis. Having been blessed with a healthy body myself, I had little real insight but could offer advice.

Several years later, I—along with my husband and two children—was involved in a head-on collision which crushed my face and necessitated nearly a year of recovery for my mangled body. Then it became *my* turn to wonder *why* and I found that it is much easier to give advice than it is to take it.

Answers are not always imminent. My personal search required several years and many tears as I tried to understand. Time has a way of mellowing the hues and developing a sense of perspective. I can now honestly say that the accident was a turning point in my life as I learned to focus on what is really important in our brief journey on this earth. Through a deeper study of the Scriptures, I learned that God must providentially work *in* us before He can work *through* us.

I have examined the promise of Romans 8:28 from every angle imaginable as I struggled with this timeless question that had now become my own: "And we know that all things work together for good to them that love God, to them who are the called according to his purpose." That passage does not claim that *everything* in a Christian's life will be good. Instead, it very quietly and powerfully asserts that everything will eventually *work together* for good. Raw eggs, shortening, and flour are repulsive in taste by themselves. When they are properly mixed and subjected to the heat of the oven, however, a very delicious cake can be produced. We may not be able to completely understand the reasons for our troubles because we do not reason as God does.

> For my thoughts are not your thoughts, neither are your ways my ways, saith the Lord. For as the heavens are higher

than the earth, so are my ways higher than your ways, and
my thoughts than your thoughts (Isa. 55:8-9).

God is not on trial; He does not have to prove Himself.
He did not place us on this earth to necessarily be free
from heartache during the years that we are here. The *only*
thing of lasting consequence is our eternal destination.

Our purpose for being on this earth is very aptly illus-
trated by the story about a parade and a young boy who
viewed it from a tiny knothole in a fence. God, in His wisdom, could see the entire event from beginning to end
whereas the boy could only see a small part. From His van-
tage point, God can see that the events which seem so terrible to us can often make the difference in our eternal
destination, which is the only thing of lasting importance.

Dilemma

The question of *why?* has echoed from the walls of time
since the beginning of civilization. Adam and Eve must
have been bewildered when Cain killed Abel. Abraham
probably had some doubts as he prepared his son Isaac for
the required sacrifice. The silence of Gethsemane was pen-
etrated by the cries and tears of the Son of God as He
pleaded for the removal of the cup of suffering which he
was about to endure. Hebrews 5:7 tells us that the Father
was able to save His Son. Why did He choose not to heed
the pleadings of Christ? The divine nature of Christ understood. The human side was perplexed.

Because we are only humans, we reason as human beings do. To us, it seems that God allows troubles to come
our way either because He is not powerful enough to prevent them or because He does not love us sufficiently to
spare us from harm.

Is God Not Powerful Enough?

Matthew 19:26 assures the child of God that "with God
all things are possible." The Father can do anything, but

He has limited Himself. It is difficult for human beings to imagine a God who obeys His own laws and the limitations which He has placed upon Himself. Hebrews 6:18 states that it is impossible for God to lie. Neither can He be tempted with evil (James 1:13). God has limited Himself in the four following ways.

First, the Father limited Himself in the garden when Adam and Eve were given the freedom of choice. In the midst of the garden were two significant trees. Eating of the tree of life would have enabled Adam and Eve to live forever (Gen. 3:22). Partaking of the fruit of the other tree would have given them power to discern good and evil (Gen. 2:17). When they chose to eat of the latter, they were cast out of the garden and removed from the possibility of eating of the tree of life and living forever (Gen. 3:22-24). At that moment the dying process began, and it continues until this day. Slowly, but surely, the body ceases to function properly until death finally takes its toll. Adam and Eve, not God, should be blamed.

Second, when Adam and Eve sinned, the laws of nature were set in force, including death-producing diseases and accidents. These laws have the inherent nature of being both good and bad, but God limited Himself when He made those laws consistent. For example, fire has benefited mankind since the early pages of history as man warmed himself by its heat and also cooked his food on its coals.

However, the laws of nature are consistent. Fire will burn anything with which it comes in contact. If my hand happens to get in its way, the fire will burn it. The same principle is true of electricity. It is beneficial to us when it lights our buildings and warms our homes, but the power charging through those wires is no respecter of persons. When used without proper precautions, it kills people, both good and evil.

Third, many of the ills of mankind can be traced to our own carelessness of the laws of nature. We do not always properly care for our own bodies and, consequently, suffer from our negligence. Instead of blaming God for allowing an automobile accident to happen, often it is we who should accept the blame for driving carelessly.

Fourth, we live in a world with other people and sometimes they are careless or just plain mean. Yet we would not want to be deprived of companionship and live the life of a hermit. Part of the price of companionship is living with others who are free to do as they please. Drunk drivers kill innocent people. Criminals harm our loved ones, but none of us would want to live devoid of other people.

By way of summary, we may say that God is all-powerful but that He placed certain limitations on Himself when He gave Adam and Eve the freedom to make their own choices. Because of their wrong choice, the aging process, with inevitable death, began. Second, the laws of nature were set in motion to work consistently for both the good and the evil if they are to be reliable. When we violate those laws, we are hurt. Third, our own carelessness of those laws causes much of our trouble. Fourth, living with others causes hardships for the innocent as well as the evil.

Does God Not Love Us?

Troubles are promised to mankind, and we cannot expect to live a life of ease. Yes, God is powerful enough to free man of all troubles; but He limited Himself when Adam and Eve were given the freedom of choice and the laws of nature became consistent.

Sometimes we need to distinguish between kindness and love. Too often we have a Santa Claus image of God. We feature Him as someone who passes out toys and candy to good little boys and girls and never disciplines in any way. Such action may be kindness, but it is not love. God's love is completely unselfish. He loved us enough to give His only begotten Son so we could have eternal life (John 3:16). Just as a good parent wants his children to develop into responsible, unspoiled adults, so does God desire the perfecting of His children. Love had rather see a child suffer in order to produce his ultimate good than withhold all discipline and watch him grow into a contemptible adult whom no one can tolerate. It is the loving parent who ignores the pleading of a child who is facing a painful injection to cause immunity from a disease. A loving parent wants whatever is best for the child.

How Troubles Make Us Better

Troubles are promised and we should expect them whether we completely understand the reasoning or not. Nevertheless, an honest examination of troubles, as seen from God's eyes, should cause us to be more accepting.

(1) *Testing is a part of the Christian life.* Examinations should be expected because they have been promised. As a teacher in public education, I never ceased to be amazed over the lack of preparation of many students when it came time for a test. Even though I had told them that they were to be tested several days in advance and even furnished sample questions for their study, some would always look at me in bewilderment on the day of the test as if they had never even heard of the material being covered.

The Christian must remember that our problems and troubles are filtered by God.

> There hath no temptation taken you but such as is common to man: but God is faithful, who will not suffer you to be tempted above that ye are able; but will with the temptation also make a way to escape, that ye may be able to bear it (1 Cor. 10:13).

Just as I daily place a filter in the coffeepot to filter out certain distasteful oils, so does God require every trouble that comes into my life to be passed through His masterful filter. Do not fret over burdens because they are indicative of God's confidence in your ability to handle them. Problems are necessary to our growth just as exercise is necessary for a baby's proper development. Each time that we successfully handle a new trouble in our lives, we climb another rung in the ladder to spiritual maturity. Each hardship should make us better instead of bitter.

A Christian does not become so perfect that testing ceases. It seems that just as soon as we satisfactorily complete one trial and breathe a sigh of relief, another one rears its ugly head and demands our attention. All too often the scar tissue never leaves, but the child of God is made stronger by each successful victory.

(2) *Troubles Cause Us to Repent and Depend upon God.* David realized that he had sinned before he was afflicted and confessed that it was good for him to have been afflicted (Ps. 119:67, 71).

Undoubtedly, the suffering of the prodigal son caused him to repent. God cannot use the proud and the haughty. "Humble yourselves in the sight of the Lord, and he shall lift you up" (James 4:10). We are told in 2 Corinthians 12:9 that Christ's strength is made perfect in weakness.

Most of us are too proud to be of much use to God. Just as the great stones that are used in making a mighty building must be cut and shaped to be of value, so must we also be cut and shaped by the master builder. Ephesians 2:10 refers to Christians as God's workmanship. How many times do we sing loudly that God is the potter and we are the clay and then whimper when God starts shaping our lives! Lives that have yielded to the master's touch become precious jewels. Remember that a pearl is the result of an oyster's irritation by a grain of sand. Slowly it secretes a substance which protects it from the pain of the sand. Layer by layer, a precious pearl is formed.

Often God wants to give us great spiritual blessings, but our hands are too full of worldly cares to receive such gifts. It is then that our hands must be emptied before they can hold the wonderful blessings which God would like to bestow upon us. Just as Christ's hands were torn by spikes before He was lifted from the earth, so must our own hands be emptied of worldly cares and be filled with burdens that will make us better before we can be lifted up.

(3) *Sometimes God Chastens Us.* God's natural laws are consistent, but often He works through these laws or by some other means to chasten His children. Note the following Scriptures:

> As a man chasteneth his son, so the Lord thy God chasteneth thee (Deut. 8:5).

> My son, despise not the chastening of the Lord; neither be weary of his correction: for whom the Lord loveth he correcteth: even as a father the son in whom he delighteth (Prov. 3:11-12).

> Behold, happy is the man whom God correcteth (Job 5:17).

> My son, despise not thou the chastening of the Lord, nor faint when thou art rebuked of him: for whom the Lord loveth he chasteneth, and scourgeth every son whom he receiveth (Heb. 12:5-6).

> Now no chastening for the present seemeth to be joyous, but grievous: nevertheless afterward it yieldeth the peaceable fruit of righteousness unto them which are exercised thereby (Heb. 12:10-11).

> As many as I love, I rebuke and chasten (Rev. 3:19).

The Scriptures quoted above could leave little doubt in the mind of the honest student that God chastens His children much as an earthly father corrects his children to make them better. We may not understand how or why, but the facts speak for themselves.

(4) *Every Tribulation Is Not the Result of Our Sin.* While the Scriptures very plainly teach that God does chasten His children to make them better, it should not be

assumed that all tribulation is an indication of a person's sin. Most of our troubles are the natural result of living in a world with consistent laws of nature and filled with other people who have the freedom to act as they wish. Christ Himself gave two such examples in Luke 13:1-5: the Galileans whose blood Pilate mingled with the sacrifices and those upon whom the tower of Siloam fell. Also the blind man in John 9:1-3 was not so afflicted because of his own sins.

(5) *Trouble Perfects Our Christian Character.* Just as a child has difficulty in understanding how a spanking, lovingly administered by a parent, can make him better in years to come, so do we sometimes lack the ability to comprehend how tribulations can make us better. "For our light affliction, which is but for a moment, worketh for us a far more exceeding and eternal weight of glory" (2 Cor. 4:17).

Just as diamonds are not polished with velvet but with abrasive elements and gold must be refined to be of use, so must our Christian characters be polished by the cares of this world. Patience, an attribute characteristic of a mature Christian life, is brought about by the trying of our faith (James 1:2-3) and by tribulation (Rom. 5:3).

Just as Moses lacked the leadership qualities needed for the deliverance of his people from bondage and had to be shaped in the crucible of Midian for forty years, so must we experience troubles before we can be of any true value in God's service. Remember that kites rise against the wind, not with it.

Perhaps the phrase, "the challenge of restrictions," best exemplifies the heart of the material presented in this section. For example, most of us would have great difficulty in even walking from one end of an ice skating rink to the other. It is the ice skating artist who can accept the challenge of gliding across the ice on very thin blades of metal while making great leaps and turns in the air. The challenge of restrictions produces the artist.

The real tragedy is not the suffering; it is going through the experiences of suffering without ever learning the lessons.

(6) *Troubles Better Enable Us to Comfort Others.* Who can best comfort a woman who has just lost her husband in death? Only a widow who has experienced the same heartache can truly penetrate the wall of suffering and give hope to a grieving heart. Only the parents of a delinquent child can give comfort to others going through a similar experience.

> Blessed be God . . . Who comforteth us in all our tribulation, that we may be able to comfort them which are in any trouble, by the comfort wherewith we ourselves are comforted of God (2 Cor. 1:3-4).

(7) *Suffering Causes Us to Gain a New Perspective in Life.* Paul admonished in Romans 8:18: "For I reckon that the sufferings of this present time are not worthy to be compared with the glory which shall be revealed in us." In this same chapter, one of the greatest eternal principles is revealed: "And we know that all things work together for good to them that love God, to them who are the called according to his purpose" (Rom. 8:28).

If we experienced only joy and pleasure in this life, we would never want to leave it for something better. When we suffer, we are lifted above the world as we learn that there is something more important and wonderful than our brief sojourn on this earth. As we long for a better life, we are gradually detached from the things of this world.

To an average family, the buying of a new car or a new house may seem very important; but the serious illness of a child in that family very quickly enables each member to view life in its proper perspective as the new car or house fades into insignificance.

Preparing for Troubles

Since the question is not "What will we do *if* troubles come?" but rather "What will we do *when* troubles come?" it is the wise Christian who gives some forethought to the inevitable. Perhaps the following suggestions will help to form a safety net.

(1) *Prepare Ahead of Time.* When a wise general was asked how his battles were won, he replied that they were won the day before! Little was left to chance.

There is a vast difference in worry and preparation. Worry is the mental attitude of continually dwelling upon something undesirable which could possibly come to pass. We practice worry until we become quite skilled in the art and it becomes an automatic reflex. Whatever we feed and exercise will grow, whether it be faith or doubt.

Instead of worrying about the future, plan for it. No person should ever learn to sail a boat in a storm. A great musician does not step out on the concert stage without many years of preparation. When we plan and practice without pressure, we can be more confident of automatic skills which take over in times of emergencies.

In planning ahead *for* troubles, we should ask ourselves the question: What is the worst thing that could happen concerning this particular problem? After we have calmly considered all possible alternatives, we should select the best course of action and file it in our subconscious minds. Then forget about it! We have made the best selection while we had a calm, reasonable mind. What else is there to do? Most of the bad things which we think might happen never materialize anyway so the odds are in our favor.

When we are not under pressure, we can depend upon the conscious part of the brain to do the reasoning. When we are under stress, however, the subconscious section of the brain takes over as it relies upon habits that were used to meet similar situations earlier in life. It is our responsibility to groove desirable traits into our brains by constant practice in order that we might take the right action without even thinking about it. This is the rationale behind fire drills and tornado practices.

(2) *Become a Dedicated Student of God's Word.* The Bible is filled with wisdom that can enable us to meet practically all of life's problems, but we do not become good students in times of stress. Instead, we carefully drop the seeds of His Word into our hearts while we *are* rational and receptive to the message. Slowly, those seeds take root and spring into our subconscious minds to guide us into the proper course of action during times of stress and troubles.

(3) *Develop Prayer Habits before Troubles Come.* The commands to pray are clear (Eph. 6:18; Phil. 4:6; 1 Thess. 5:17). Our prayers should be according to God's will (1 John 5:14) and must be asked in faith (James 1:6).

Just as we do not learn how to sail a boat in a storm, neither should we *try* to learn how to pray during a crisis. We must already have a deep and abiding friendship with God, one that enables us to talk with Him about any problem that may come into our lives. We should understand that sometimes God's answer apparently is "Yes." On other occasions His reply must be: "No, it is not best." All too often we are made to realize that His answer evidently is: "It is not yet time." Instead of going to God in prayer with orders for our wishes, we should pray that we will be channels for whatever is best.

As we pray, we should realize that God is by our side during trials in four ways.

First, never forget the power of the Word of God. So many of our problems could be put in their proper perspective if only we would take the time to fathom the riches of inspiration. The answers are there. We have simply failed to read the instructions (2 Tim. 3:16).

Second, God works through natural means. Just as the good Samaritan used the medicinal qualities of oil and wine as he ministered to the injured man (Luke 10:34), so does God work through medical means as well as through counselors and other human beings in dealing with life's problems. It is wrong to pray for healing and then refuse medical help. It is using poor judgment to ask God to heal a troubled marriage while shunning the counsel of a Christian friend.

Third, God works providentially. How many times has a person fully recovered after the doctors had already admitted that they had done all they could do? The providential care of His children's lives is not the same as the miraculous gifts that were imparted to the early Christians. Those gifts were given in a special way for the purpose of confirming the message of the new revelation from God, and they only lasted for a special length of time (1 Cor. 13:10; James 1:25). While God no longer works through Christians by means of miracles He still works providentially in our lives. Otherwise, prayer would be useless; we would only need good doctors and medicine in times of sickness.

In the Old Testament God promised His special care to His people if they obeyed Him (Lev. 26:3-13). The wise writer of Proverbs admonished: "In all thy ways acknowledge him, and he shall direct thy paths" (Prov. 3:6).

The Scriptures abound with examples of God's providential working in the lives of His children.

Abraham's servant was able to identify Jehovah's selection of a bride for Isaac by the chosen maiden's offer to also draw water for the camels (Gen. 24:14,19). Mordecai observed of Queen Esther: "Who knoweth whether thou art come to the kingdom for such a time as this" (Esther 4:14)? The normal misfortunes in Joseph's life were intended by God to work together for good to save His people (Gen. 50:20).

The New Testament further assures God's children that they will be under His watchful care:

> But seek ye first the kingdom of God, and his righteousness; and all these things shall be added unto you (Matt. 6:33).

> Lo, I am with you alway, even unto the end of the world (Matt. 28:20).

> But my God small supply all your need according to his riches in glory by Christ Jesus (Phil. 4:19).

> Now unto him that is able to do exceeding abundantly above all that we ask or think, according to the power that worketh in us (Eph. 3:20).

> For the eyes of the Lord are over the righteous, and his ears are open unto their prayers (1 Pet. 3:12).

> There hath no temptation taken you but such as is common to man: but God is faithful, who will not suffer you to be tempted above that ye are able; but will with the temptation also make a way to escape, that ye may be able to bear it (1 Cor. 10:13).

Today we make our requests known to the Father (Phil. 4:6-7) and then trust in His providential care to do what is best.

Fourth, God gives us sufficient grace to deal with our problems. Paul prayed three times for God to remove an affliction that he called a thorn in the flesh and was told instead: "My grace is sufficient for thee" (2 Cor. 12:7-9).

There will be times when heartaches, accidents, diseases, and other trials will come our way. Sometimes, despite our pleadings, God chooses not to change our circumstances, either by His providence or by working through natural means.

The Father did not remove the cross from Christ but instead gave His Son the strength to endure it. We must also at times beg for God's grace to withstand our trials. Through it all, we become *stronger.*

(4) *Develop a Deep Trust in God.* Just as a turbulent sea leaves the deepest part of the ocean undisturbed, so should troubles fail to shatter the inner core of a Christian. Once I cut my finger and wore a bandage for several days. When I was doing some writing with a pen, I removed the bandage but found that the finger was still too sore to hold the pen. Replacing the bandage, I found that I could still write without pain. What was the difference? The pen was still there, just the same. My finger still had its soreness, but now I had something to shield me. God is our shield in times of trouble. He will be there to protect us. It is a wise Christian who is aware of God's protection and who remembers His guidance through previous times of troubles. Slowly but surely an undoubting faith emerges, reassuring us that He always has been our helper and will always be by our side, regardless of whatever trouble may come our way.

(5) *Cultivate Christian Friendships.* Most Christians who successfully cope with real problems in life readily admit that they would not have made it without Christian friends by their sides. Deep and abiding friendships are not made on the spur of the moment, but rather years of cultivation are required as they are formed layer upon layer of common experiences. The wise writer of Ecclesiastes wrote:

> Two are better than one ... For if they fall, the one will lift up his fellow: but woe to him that is alone when he falleth; for he hath not another to help him up (Eccles. 4:9-10).

Every Christian rightfully turns to God in prayer, but we are humans and we need another human with whom to exchange words and understanding glances. Only a Christian can have the same set of standards as the child of God.

Christ Himself knew the value of Christian friendship. Twelve men were selected as His companions for three years. Just as we feel closer to some of our friends than to others, so did Christ feel closer to Peter, James, and John. One of the primary values of Christian friendships is the manner in which such companions act as conductors of our feelings. Troubles will come to all of us. As long as they flow through us, little harm will be done. Friends are to our emotional houses as good conductors are to the house in which we live. Sometimes they prevent the house from burning down.

Methods of Coping

Problems are inevitable. We should make plans before trials come our way. When problems rear their ugly heads, how do we cope?

(1) *Learn to Properly Express Feelings.* Christ was the Son of God living in a human body. If He went through such agony in the garden that an angel from Heaven was sent to strengthen Him (Luke 22:43), why should we feel shame when we have trouble accepting hardships? There is nothing wrong with admitting that we are bewildered and confused. Such an action can be a wonderful catharsis for our emotions. Steam from a teakettle can either make it sing or explode.

(2) *Bear Only One Day's Burdens at a Time.* Most of us struggle down the road of life with three heavy sacks upon our backs: yesterday's cares wrapped in heavy blankets of guilt for failure to have done better; today's burdens; and tomorrow's imagined troubles. There is

small wonder that we stay tired all the time. We must forget yesterday, quit worrying about tomorrow, and shoulder only the responsibilities of today.

(3) *Deal with the Problem Itself.* There are three ways to handle a problem once it comes our way.

    (a) Sometimes it is best to meet the problem head-on. Admit what the adversity is and pull from your subconscious mind your preplanned course of action.

    (b) We must learn to wait when other problems come our way. Waiting involves bending a little bit as we patiently bide our time until better days come along.

    (c) Some problems cannot be met head-on. Waiting for better circumstances is futile. If the circumstances cannot be changed, then the Christian will just have to change attitudes and rise above tribulations. Rising above the circumstances, or sublimation, has been the catalyst for causing most victorious people to become high achievers in life, despite seemingly insurmountable difficulties. Remember that affliction may color our lives, but we can choose the colors.

(4) *Develop the Habit of Helping Others.* Helping has a healing effect. We all need minds with windows instead of mirrors as we turn our thoughts outward. Galatians 6:2 admonishes us to bear one another's burdens. Instead of sitting at home and crying over our own troubles, we develop our spiritual muscles by helping another person shoulder part of his load.

(5) *Find the Good in Every Problem.* We read Romans 8:28: "And we know that all things work together for good to them that love God," but we only window shop. We don't really buy the passage. All too often when we are faced with problems, there is the tendency to retreat to former days which can be no more. Instead

of mentally running back and forth, we should realize that there comes a time when some bridges must
be burned behind us because circumstances can never
be as they once were. Before we leave the site of the
burned bridge, it is wise to *sift* through the ashes.
There we will find precious nuggets of gold: The Lessons We Learned. These we should tuck close to our
hearts so they will never be lost before turning our
steps toward the future. It is at that time when we
must realize that the *end* of the road is but a *bend* in
the road. The road does go on and is smoother. It can
be the very best part of life as our hand figuratively
slips into His protective hand: "I the Lord . . . will
hold thine hand" (Isaiah 42:6).

3

Church Involvement: How Shall I Be Involved?

Irene C. Taylor

Introduction

Christianity is to be a life of service. This service is to be rendered to God above, to our fellow man, and to self. In order to render acceptable service to God, one must *belong* to His church. Even in our secular organizations one is not considered a member in good standing who merely has his name on the roll. More will be said about this later. It is by contributing of our time and talents that we become of real value to any cause. The same is true of the church of our Lord.

Further, to be a true asset to any given organization one must follow not only the entrance requirements but abide by the rules of operation. Never is this more vital than in our involvement with the church for which Christ died.

The command to be involved is personal. Each of us has an individual responsibility to be a worthy workman for the Lord. Paul through the inspiration of the Holy Spirit reveals that we are to "work out *your own* salvation with fear and trembling" (Phil. 2:12, emphasis supplied).

It has often been observed that *I* is in the middle of sin meaning that *I* am in the middle of every sin charged to my account. Let it here be noted that *I* is the beginning of involvement. The elders of the congregation have the responsibility to plan a challenging program of work but in order for that program to succeed it requires the cooperation of the entire membership, including me.

There is no way to fathom the amount of good which could be accomplished to *God's* glory if every member of the church were as enthusiastically involved in the work of his/her local congregation as many are in secular/civic organizations.

Matthew records the parable of the talents (Matt. 25:14-30). Recall that the dispersing of the talents was according to each one's ability (v. 15). The five-talent man accepted his responsibility and put his talents to work. By so doing he was able to gain five talents more. The two-talent man did likewise. However, the one-talent man merely buried his talent, making no effort to utilize what he was given to gain more. The Lord was pleased with the first two but greatly disappointed in the latter.

> Thou wicked and slothful servant, thou knewest that I reap where I sowed not, and gather where I have not strawed: Thou oughtest therefore to have put my money to the exchangers, and then at my coming I should have received mine own with usury. Take therefore the talent from him, and give it unto him which hath ten talents . . . And cast ye the unprofitable servant into outer darkness: there shall be weeping and gnashing of teeth (Matt. 25:26-30).

Question: Which of these servants would we be most like? The lesson we must learn here is twofold: (1) The Lord does not expect more from us than we are capable of doing and (2) He does expect us to develop and use the abilities we have been given. Reflect on the parable carefully. Those who used their talents met with the Lord's approval and were rewarded generously for their work. But the man who was satisfied to do nothing and then tried to excuse that lack of action was handed a severe punishment and the loss of his one talent.

What we do not use, we lose. It is a sobering thought to understand that we will give an account of our *failure* to utilize our abilities for His cause. We may never realize our full potential unless we try. In the day of judgment each of us will give account of "himself to God" (Rom. 14:12). The judgment meted at that great day will be "according to that he hath done, whether it be good or bad" (2 Cor. 5:10).

There is no community pool of good works from which one may draw to enhance his personal account. Each of us must answer the call to be involved—personally. Note carefully the individual scope of the following Scriptures. When not specifically stated, *you* is the understood subject by rules of grammar.

> Pure religion and undefiled before God and the Father is this, To visit the fatherless and widows in their affliction, and to keep himself unspotted from the world (James 1:27).

> Therefore, my beloved brethren, be ye stedfast, unmoveable, always abounding in the work of the Lord, forasmuch as ye know that your labour is not in vain in the Lord (1 Cor. 15:58).

> For God is not unrighteous to forget your work and labour of love, which ye have shewed toward his name, in that ye have ministered to the saints, and do minister (Heb. 6:10).

In 2 Peter 1:5-7 we find a command to add specific traits to our foundation of faith. Once again the individual directive is given: "Add to *your* faith" (emphasis supplied). Often referred to as the octave of the soul, this passage depicts the ascendancy of spiritual growth. Each step builds on the previous one(s): To faith we are to add virtue, knowledge, temperance, patience, godliness, brotherly kindness, and charity or love. These are needed to equip us in our service to the Master. Closely akin is the fruit of the Spirit with its attributes of love, joy, peace, longsuffering, gentleness, goodness, faith, meekness, and temperance (Gal. 5:22).

Just as *I* is the beginning of involvement, thereby revealing the dire need for me to be busily engaged, so is *I* scattered throughout responsibility. There is no way for me to escape my own responsibility and remain *pleasing to* God. The attitude of "Why don't *they?*" instead of "Why don't *I?*" is a plague constantly present in the church. Unless and until each of us understands and accepts our personal responsibility to participate and carry our share of the workload, we will never accomplish what we have the potential of doing.

Perhaps it would be well just here to pause and observe the need for us to understand what the work of the church actually is. The waters have been greatly muddied by those clamoring for change in the mission and worship of the church. The Bible declares that we are to preach to or teach the lost (Matt. 28:19-20; Mark 16:15-16). We are to exhort and reprove the saved that they may remain saved (Heb. 3:13; 2 Tim. 4:2). We are to practice benevolence (James 1:27; Gal. 6:10). Contrary to the view of some today, there is not a fourth work in which we are to engage as the church—entertainment. Thousands of precious dollars have been and are being spent to build gymnasiums wherein members may exercise. Instructors are sometimes brought in to teach crafts and drama in order to expand "social skills." The argument is that we need to minister to the "whole man." Absent is any authority from the Bible to engage in such. These things fall under the jurisdiction of the home and not the church. The fact that the home may not be providing such does not transfer the responsibility to the church. Let us be certain that we involve ourselves only in church activities which are authorized by God. Serving Him and His Cause must ever be our goal. We must not burden the church with that which hinders its performance of its assigned mission.

Involvement: An Opportunity to Set a Proper Example

Keeping ever in mind that we are to ascertain the scripturalness of a work before participating, we must therefore perform the acid test. "What does the Bible say?" or "Do we have Bible authority for this?" is not out of style! We are in the crucial position of leading the way toward promoting more fully the *legitimate* work of the church and weeding out the unauthorized activities being introduced.

It seems appropriate here to offer a word of encouragement to the wives of elders and preachers. Being a preacher's wife myself, the remarks may appear geared more to the wives of preachers but they are appropriate for consideration by the wives of elders as well. All too often I am hearing words of resentment from those in these roles. It is felt that they are viewed unfairly and that the expectations placed upon them should not be theirs to bear. Sadly, some objections are justified. A double standard *is* in existence. They *are* expected to live by a standard seldom applied to other church members. We seem to fail to understand that there is a high standard of living, above that of the world, for *all* Christians to observe. And our children should be taught to observe certain standards because this is how *Christians* conduct themselves and not because they are the children of elders or preachers. Constantly instilling in them that they abstain from certain types of conduct and activities because of their father breeds resentment toward him. Such is totally unfair and should be avoided with diligence. The fact that not all Christians observe such standards is a sad reality but it does not negate my responsibility to do so. Above all, we must not lower our standard or that of our children just so they can be like all the rest! We must govern our involvement with reasonableness and fairness.

On the higher plane, let me suggest to the groups mentioned above that we view our position for what it really is—an opportunity instead of an obligation. Too many times we hear the concept, "They hired my husband; they did not hire me!" This is true. However, because you are his wife you have the special *privilege* of showing the beauty of involvement in the work of the church. Whether one thinks it is fair or not, the preacher's wife can either lead the *way* toward greater involvement or she can be a millstone of hindrance to every undertaking. The fact remains, right or wrong, that it is the exception, not the rule, when the women of a congregation are actually involved in spite of the apathy of the preacher's wife. Enthusiastic elders' wives can make a noticeable difference as well.

Let me hasten to state that it is unwise for the preacher's wife to try to do it all. A good leader delegates duties. An exceptional leader organizes and trains workers so as to involve as many as possible in any given project or program. Workers need to learn how to carry on should the leader be absent. Preachers, their wives and children do sometimes become ill just as do other members. It is unfair to expect one person—usually the preacher's wife—to do it all, not only to her but also to the many members whose talent should be utilized. Many are reluctant to *volunteer* for a task but are more than willing to participate if *invited* to do so. Forget the fact that no member should have to be invited to help with a good work. Face reality, swallow your frustration, and encourage them to have a part.

Titus 2 enjoins upon the older women to "teach the young women" (v. 4). Verse 3 says the aged women are to be "teachers of good things." Certainly one of those "good things" should be to encourage (both verbally and by example) the active involvement in the work of the church. As an extra observation, should not the older women be showing the young preacher's wife by example *and* teaching?

Involvement in Good Works

For any program to succeed there must be the participation and support of dedicated workers. In the church such involvement begins with becoming a part of the membership by obedience to the Lord's invitation. This should be followed immediately with regular, dedicated attendance at all public services. This includes worship services, both morning and evening, gospel meetings, and all Bible classes. This is a commitment which the Christian makes at conversion. Failure to honor it becomes a real hindrance in becoming involved in good works.

Too often we see reflected the attitude that if it is not something big we are not interested in having a part. We seem to forget that it is the small "behind the scenes" tasks which insure the success of any project. The final result is possible only because of willing workers along the way. The Bible tells us that if we function only for the praise of men (to be seen of men) we have the wrong motive (Matt. 6:1ff). We need more Christians with the character of brother C. M. Pullias. He was among those considered as speaker for the first famous Ryman Auditorium meeting. Instead, brother N. B. Hardeman was selected. Rather than becoming offended and refusing to have any part, he stated he would be willing to sweep the floors to help the endeavor be successful. He cheerfully accepted the role of song leader when asked.

Special encouragement is hereby offered to the young wives of preachers. Be on guard against becoming jealous of the attention given your husband. Like many secular professionals he will be in the limelight often. That is required for him to function properly in his work. Turn a deaf ear to those who invite you to a pity party because you, too, are not in the spotlight! Instead, expend your energies in an area worthwhile wherein you feel comfortable and hone your skills and talents there. There is always a place for one willing to work. Many a preacher's wife has filled a real need in the field of hospitality. There is a real service to be performed by organizing the schedule for visiting speakers. Take the lead in inviting members into your home. Entertaining need not be elaborate—only warm and sincere. Even if the invitations are never reciprocated, you are still the winner. You gain a more personal association with fellow Christians. Remember the admonition of the wise man, "A man that hath friends must shew himself friendly" (Prov. 18:24). You are in position to set a standard of hospitality for others to emulate. Do not pass up the opportunity.

A word of caution should also be given. There may be situations where the preacher and his family are over-loaded. There will always be those who feel secure in their lethargy because, after all, the preacher and his wife have been employed to handle everything! Sometimes it is as-sumed that you are available to operate a free taxi service at all hours or that your home is open for their use in en-tertaining socially at their convenience. You are justified in refusing to be used unfairly. When you allow such to happen, you are hurting not only yourself, but also those attempting to abuse your time as well.

Especially vital is the need to maintain *family* time and, more so, the care and training of your small children. The rearing of children is a very vital part of a mother's church work! The command to "train up a child in the way he should go" is to the mother of the preacher's children as much as to any other mother! And those who rob you of time to accomplish that goal will be the first to criticize you for a job poorly done. When we neglect our children, even to be of service to the congregation, we are playing a dangerous game. *Our* children have the right to stable home life, too. Do not be caught in the trap of leaving your chil-dren with first one and another to meet the whims of the membership. Each of us will want to do our part to help those in need because we are *Christians*.

There are many areas of involvement open to women and this includes the preacher's wife and the elders' wives. Women are by nature equipped to teach young children. Though there are exceptions (my husband is one) most men are not as comfortable working with little children as are women. It is sad that most women shy away from using their talents here, even when young. Young mothers have the mistaken idea that they should not teach classes in which their children are involved. (This exception never is applied to the preacher's wife.) In reality, children do bet-ter with one familiar to them. It should be no real problem to control the conduct of our own children if they are controlled at home. Little children are so receptive to teaching. They are also so active. For this reason, *young* mothers need to be willing to work out a schedule for teaching nursery and preschool classes. Children's classes, those of primary school age, respond better to women teachers as a general rule.

Women *need* to be teaching a class of girls! When the potential for such a class is present, it is ideal to begin a separate class for girls by junior high age. In our society much of the dating concept has already been formed by this age. Sadly, parents are pushing our young people into adult situations before they are mature enough emotionally to handle them. A *dedicated Christian woman* should be encouraged to teach biblical concepts for dating and marriage. Our girls have been sold a dangerous bill of goods by the feminists. We are failing miserably to counteract their propaganda. While it is recognized that such teaching should be *instilled* in the home and *reinforced* in our Bible classes, the fact remains that it is not! It is also a fact that a girl may feel more comfortable in confiding in a Bible class teacher with whom she has a close relationship than in her own mother. (Our boys need to have a similar class taught by a dedicated Christian man. They need to be trained in the art of being a good husband and father. For some time it has been of concern to this writer that a training class for boys usually is limited to training for participation in the worship. They need to know how to treat the opposite sex in dating and marriage, too!)

Through teaching women's classes much good can be accomplished. Women feel more free to discuss issues pertinent to them when in a class void of men. It is satisfying to see more women willingly taking the challenge to teach publicly. A ladies' class is a fine way to develop the ability to teach publicly. Some have discovered an ability to teach beyond the local classroom and we welcome good, sound women teachers. The recent trend toward having special "ladies' day" programs can be a good thing—*if* we are careful to have sound speakers do the teaching. Congregations should exercise the same care for this type of program that should be exercised in securing a man speaker for meeting work. Such a program should be done—always—with the approval of the eldership. There are those who speak at "ladies' day" programs who promote the push for an expanded role for women in the church. These should be given *no forum* to spout their false philosophy. Some sessions seem more a promotion of social skills, fancy entertainment, and fashion shows. A Bible program should spotlight the *Bible* with in-depth teaching of Bible truths. We women can do much to strengthen the teaching program of the congregation or we can help weaken it by demanding innovations unauthorized by God's Word. May we always do the former and never the latter.

Visitation is another area crying for more involvement. Every congregation has a number of widows, widowers, and shut-ins. These spend lonely hours with no one to share their emptiness. An occasional visit would mean so much to them. Sometimes that visit needs to go beyond a social call. James writes, "Pure religion and undefiled before God and the Father is this, to visit the fatherless and widows in their affliction, and to keep himself unspotted from the world" (James 1:27). "In their affliction" means when there is a need for help. We women should be able to observe such and readily respond to the need. It is not difficult to notice when dishes need washing, a refrigerator needs defrosting, or a floor swept and cleaned. None of us should consider ourselves above providing such services. There are always those who face trials and discouragements. A shoulder to lean on could make a big difference. Our young people face many temptations and discouragements. A word of caring and encouragement can provide the strength needed to stay on the right path. Jesus said, "For whosoever shall give you a cup of water to drink in my name because ye belong to Christ, verily I say unto you, he shall not lose his reward" (Mark 9:41; Matt. 10:42).

In the Ripley congregation we have in place a schedule of committees composed of women willing to provide food whenever there is a need. Overseen capably by a deacon's wife, it is the best organized service group with which I have had the privilege of working. Its pattern of operation permits wide participation and has filled a need in many circumstances which before would have been overlooked.

Sending flowers or items of cheer in the name of the church to those hospitalized and those in bereavement has opened many a door. At the least, it expresses the love and concern which Christians have one for the other. A woman can fill this role with proficiency.

Also in our local congregation we have a number who have adopted our shut-ins. The thrust is to visit, send cards and/or gifts on special occasions such as birthdays, and in general show that these are not forgotten. For some, we are the only family available.

Personal work is another avenue open for women to become involved. There are those whom we can influence that the preacher might never be able to reach. Consider the account of the Samaritan women in John 4. Here we have related the story of a woman who had lived a less than exemplary life. Yet she invited her friends to "come, see a man, which told me all things that ever I did: is not this the Christ" (v. 29)? We are often reluctant to invite our friends to attend worship with us or to study the Bible together. There is an art to turning a conversation to things spiritual that many of us have failed to develop.

The Value of Involvement

Very little is gained from membership in any given organization which results in passive participation. This is readily recognized by secular organizations. Miss a given number of meetings without cause and the membership in these is terminated. Yet one church member who is active in such a civic organization expressed resentment because

the elders and preacher of this local congregation stress
the importance of regular, dedicated worship attendance!
We need to learn to differentiate between service to man
and service to God and appreciate the vast difference in
the value of each. Without dedicated service to God and
His church we will find our name removed from the heavenly roll come Judgment Day.

Merely belonging provides one with no personal satisfaction. The haphazard manner of many who profess to be
Christians brings them more misery than happiness. When
Christians only occasionally attend worship services, they
miss the opportunity to refuel, grow, and show publicly the
beauty of true devotion to God. An elderly Christian lady,
blind, deaf, and now unable to walk, insisted that her family continue to bring her to worship services regularly. When
asked why, she replied, "I want folks to know whose side I
am on." She realized the value of wielding *good* influence.
The attitude of merely belonging is the attitude that ex-
udes the "Why don't *they*?" instead of "Why don't *we*?" concept. It is the attitude of "Why don't *you*?" instead of "May
I?" alluded to earlier in this study. One never feels the personal responsibility as long as he stays in the "they" mode
of thinking.

Good works are to be a natural part of the Christian
life. We are to abound in every good work (1 Cor. 15:58).
Luke records that Jesus went about doing good (Acts 10:38).
To be like Him we must be willing to do good as well. In
Acts 9:36 we read of the good works of Tabitha. We are told
that "this woman was full of good works and almsdeeds
which she did" (v. 39). There is no hint that she was a
wealthy woman. Rather she used her talents to utilize what
she had and shared with others. We cannot be excused from
involvement in good works because we have not amassed
great wealth. The greatest gift we can give is first to give
of self and then our time and talents. We will then have
the satisfaction of knowing we have helped another along
life's way.

Our purpose in this life is to prepare for Heaven in eternity and to make this world a better place now and for posterity. Our involvement in upholding the work of the church is needed to insure its success. The influence of our good works should be done through the church to God's glory. We greatly err when we expend our energy through secular avenues, bringing the crumbs of our time and talent to the Lord. The excuse that "I work" will not hold water in the final judgment. God's work must come *first.* First means number one and must not be displaced by even number two—one's family. Each must be kept in proper perspective. The exhilaration of knowing that one has had a part in saving not only one's soul but the souls of others is reward in and of itself. Involvement produces a feeling of accomplishment. We all have a need to feel we belong, and that feeling can be met in the spiritual realm by our willingness to be totally committed to promoting God's cause and working for its growth.

Conclusion

Someone has observed that woman is the greatest untapped resource in the church. There is much we can do for the Lord if we will overcome the attitude that we must be in a public capacity in order to serve. Remember, the behind-the-scenes worker is really the backbone of any program. Let us never allow ourselves to become dissatisfied with God's pattern. When we do, we become a tool of the devil.

Get involved in the work program of your local congregation. Work under the leadership of godly elders. There is no mandatory age of retirement. We need the wisdom of age as well as the vigor of youth. In the words of the cross-stitch plaque: The wages may not be great, but the retirement is out of this world. "And let us not be weary in well doing: for in due season we shall reap, if we faint not" (Gal. 6:9).

PART TWO

Marriage

4

Intimacy
LeAnn Duke

The Purity and Purpose of Marriage

Bombarded by the sexual exploitations available at every turn, women and men are disillusioned, misled, and confused about the subject of intimacy. Sexual love has been from the beginning a gift from God, but men have done all within their power to contaminate it. What God made to be a beautiful and wonderful expression of feelings between a man and his wife has been turned into something vulgar and repulsive to many. With the making and selling of erotic movies and pornographic magazines and other vile abuses men and women have become twisted in their thinking of what is good and bad, right and wrong. Anything seems to be okay today. To be open minded means freedom of expression through any means available: writings, photography, art, music, or sexuality. They do what feels good. There seems to be no shame when two people sleep together before they are married. Homosexuality and lesbianism are openly accepted as alternatives to God's plan for one man and one woman for life. The sexual roles of mankind have been distorted, and many young people marry without a clear view of what is expected in the bonds of this marital relationship. Inexperience leads them to believe that the passions that burn so intensely in youth need only to be satisfied. This, to them, is the ultimate experience. Lust for gratification ignores the joy of the satisfying fulfillment that intimacy brings to the union of marriage. Intimacy involves much more than merely satisfying the sexual urges. God intended for a man and his wife to be intimate friends and lovers.

God designed man and woman to be sexual creatures. The very structure of the human body indicates that God had in mind intimacy between men and women. The Genesis account of creation confirms this fact when God created His final handiwork and brought her to Adam. And God said, "Therefore a man shall leave his father and mother and be joined to his wife, and they shall become one flesh" (Gen. 2:24). Adam knew that God had given him a very special gift. He knew that, though she was created from his rib, she was created to complete him as a human being. Adam was to love and care for his new wife. He was to respect her as an individual, realizing that she would bring a fulfillment to his existence that none of God's other creatures had.

God designed within Adam and Eve a sexual desire and therefore mankind has the God-conceived, God-authorized, and God-sanctioned idea of sexual pleasure. God gave mankind the emotional capacity for sexual love. He created our bodies to respond to sexual arousal and He expected it to be fulfilled in marriage.

Some women have, perhaps innocently, been mislead about their roles in fulfilling the sexual needs of their husbands and having their own needs met as well. Many young women go into the marriage relationship knowing only the basics about the delights of sexual love. They may have received little training due to embarrassment or the lack of knowledge on the part of their mothers. Some enter marriage with the idea that the husband will demand his conjugal rights and there is nothing that can prevent it. They may have been taught that one just suffers through it. Some enter marriage totally ignorant of the act of marriage and believe that their husbands will know just what to do. This is a travesty. Sexual love was meant to be shared, and both the husband and the wife should be willing to help each other to reach their full enjoyment.

Since this is a book primarily for women, I will not attempt to undertake the responsibilities or the negligence of some men. Not unkindly, we must admit that there are many men who do not know how to please their wives nor do they care to learn. There are also many men who do not love or respect their wives as they should. Reality is that there are many men who abuse their roles as leaders in the home and take no thought to giving or sharing anything in their relationship with their wives. Some men are drunks and are rough and uncaring and could be unfaithful to their wives. Some are physically abusive and daily threaten the wives' safety. Others may be verbally abusive, completely tearing down the confidence of their spouses and making them feel worthless. This obviously does not encourage or enhance the sexual response of the women to their husbands. Neither my knowledge nor space will permit me to delve into the "why's" of such behavior. I will attempt to briefly touch on a few things that can enhance the sexual relationship. These can also make the Christian couple who desire a happy marriage intensely satisfied, enabling them to know a little heaven on earth.

Intimacy involves two. It implies the sharing of many things, not just mutual sexual satisfaction. Sharing requires giving more than fifty-fifty. When a couple shares the most private part of themselves with one another, they must be able to communicate their thoughts, ideas, plans, and their desires. Honesty is a necessity. When two cannot be honest with each other, the relationship will suffer. A young woman once told me that she rarely was able to totally appreciate intercourse because she was afraid to really let go and enjoy herself. She was self-conscious about her body, her expressions, and how she was viewed by her husband during their lovemaking. This fear and lack of trust and being completely honest began to put a strain on their sex life.

He could sense her discomfort and began to think there was a more serious problem. Finally she let her guard down and admitted that she was afraid to be completely free with him for fear he would laugh at her. This, he assured her, was not true. From the day she recognized the truth and admitted her fear to her husband, their love life has been wonderful for them both.

The husband and wife must be able to fully trust each other. They should never attempt to use the sexual relationship to manipulate or to take advantage of each other (1 Cor. 7:4-5). This shows an immaturity that has no place in marriage. But most importantly it is a sin. The sexual relationship can enhance and bring out the best in the person you love. It can give your mate confidence in himself and help him to attain his goals.

Communication in the bedroom should always be maintained. You should not be afraid to tell or show your husband what you like. Tell him what feels good and what doesn't feel good. Loving husbands want to know what excites their wives. Many times what seems to be a major problem can be solved very quickly if we will just be brave enough to tactfully and kindly say what bothers us. If there is a touch or lovemaking act that disturbs you or makes you feel uncomfortable, then he should know about it. If a certain sexual touch that you enjoyed in the past is no longer pleasurable, you should tell him. He will only know what you have told him before and the pleasure you have experienced in the past. Ignoring the uncomfortable feelings will only bring about your unwillingness to be intimate. The longer you keep your discomfort hidden from him, the more it will hurt him. And if he senses your unwillingness, he may also begin to dread the act of lovemaking because he may feel he cannot please you. Honesty will make you both much better lovers. Your husband will continue to feel comfortable and confident as your lover.

You might say, "But telling my husband something negative about his lovemaking will crush him. Even if I am trying to make it better, he will take it personally." For the relationship to be what it should be, the man has to be mature enough and love you enough to want to help you to achieve the highest form of pleasure from your lovemaking. And he should respect, admire, and love you more for being honest and for being willing to help him please you. Most husbands are thrilled to know their wives want an exciting sex life. But remember that intimacy is a two-way street. As a wife, you should be willing to seek to please your husband. If your husband has a specific request of you and wishes to show you how to please him, be a willing partner. Be flexible. This does not mean that bizarre or unnatural acts are acceptable. But a loving wife should always be ready and anxious to learn different methods of normal sexual acts so she can fully satisfy her husband's desires.

Don't be afraid to be sexy. God made your body to be pleasing to your husband and there is nothing shameful about revealing yourself to your mate. Remember how you took such time and care with your appearance while you were dating? Has it changed over the years? Marriage does not give license to become a slob. Before marriage and just shortly after we would have never thought about greeting our love at the door in some ragged pair of pajamas or our favorite threadbare nightgown we slept in the night before. We would never have thought to greet him with teeth unbrushed, or with greasy, unwashed, or unkempt hair. During the dating period and early marriage to this man, we did all the things we knew he liked. We attempted in every possible way to impress him. We cooked special meals, we tidied the house, we made sure that his happiness was our main priority. Many women greet their husbands at the door in their gowns or bathrobe, not because they have any intention of enticing or seducing him, but because they have been dressed like that since they got up that morning. They have not touched their hair with a brush or done a thing to make themselves attractive for the man they say they love and desire. Sound appealing? What if the reverse were true? How would we feel if we worked the nine to five and daily came home only to be greeted as we come in the door by a guy dressed in his torn boxer shorts and dirty, rumpled T-shirt, unshaven, with bad breath, and unkempt in every other way? Would we be glad to be home each evening? Would we be inclined to be attentive and interested in someone who was not interested in himself?

Here are some simple things that any woman can implement in her daily routine that do not cause a great expense or take much time.

1. *Dress neatly each day.* Bathe, put makeup on, and choose clean, pressed clothes. Also, choose frequently an outfit in which you know your husband thinks you look great. This should immediately attract his attention.

2. *Fix his favorite meal and put candles on the table.* This can set the tone for a peaceful, comfortable atmosphere that may simply lead to a night of much-needed conversation. This can also easily set the mood for warm and wonderful sexual fulfillment.

3. *Write your husband love notes* and hide them in various places where you know he will find them: underwear drawer, briefcase, desk at the office, desk at home (if he has one), lunchbox, checkbook, or bathroom mirror. Use your imagination!

4. *Stop occasionally at the card section* in your favorite variety store or drug store and pick out an intimate card that says something that you find particularly difficult to express or one that just simply says, "I love you." This is a wonderful way to express yourself and communicate your needs or desires to your husband.

5. *When funds allow, pack an overnight bag for both of you.* Call a hotel or motel and make one night's reservation. Check with trustworthy friends or neighbors and see if they will keep your children (if you have any) for the night. Make a deal that you will keep their children one night in exchange for keeping yours one night. Plan to pick up your husband from work (if you have two cars) and kidnap him, taking him away for a night for just the two of you. If you only have one car, then have everything ready and spirit him away as soon as he arrives home. Again be flexible. Check to make sure he doesn't have prior commitments so that you are not disappointed if plans do not work out.

6. *Don't be afraid to dress sexy for your husband.* He loves to know that you want to please him. There is nothing shameful about dressing to entice your man. The shameful thing is when women no longer care if they entice or interest their husbands. Make an effort to wear colors he likes. If at all possible, choose perfumes or colognes that he finds irresistible. If your budget allows, go shopping for a new piece of lingerie. Trade in that old flannel nightgown for something a little more interesting.

7. *Be feminine.* There is nothing more unsexy than a woman who attempts to be as tough as a man, whether it be in her dress, her speech, or her job. God made us soft and gentle. We are to be ready to comfort him. We are to be the weaker vessel. There is nothing nicer than to know that your husband wants to lessen your burdens. Many women resent this and therefore attempt to show their strength in a way that is contrary to what God planned. Man was created to be the stronger one and the woman is to allow him to be so. So don't be afraid to be soft and sexy.

8. *Learn to enjoy touching your mate.* Holding hands, soft caresses and kisses are what ignited the flame in the first place. When was the last time you massaged your husband's back when it wasn't hurting? Try to remind yourself to touch more often. If it has been a while since you touched your mate, other than accidentally, give it a try. You and he might both be surprised!

9. *Don't be afraid to be a sexually aggressive wife.* This lets your husband know that you still desire him and you need his lovemaking. The woman who occasionally approaches her husband might be surprised at the intensity of their lovemaking in contrast with her husband always being the aggressor.

10. *Don't be afraid to surrender sexually to your husband.* "A woman is the only creature that can conquer by surrendering."[4] Learn to be comfortable with yourself and allow yourself to have fun. The closeness God intended for husband and wife is good and right. Surrendering your body to your husband can give you a fulfillment like no other. It takes time and patience, but don't give up. It's worth it!

If we are willing to learn to "cultivate the appetite for passionate loving,"[5] then it is most probable that we will have a satisfying relationship with our mate. It is for sure that we will be pleasing to God. He created us and gave us a beautiful privilege as women to fulfill and compliment man. If we fail our husbands, we are failing ourselves and our duty to God.

The woman who wishes to please God in her marriage can know what her role is by studying God's Word. You might say, "Where do I find anything about intimacy in the Bible?" Genesis 18:12 gives us an inside look at Sarah's

---

[4] Tim and Beverly LaHaye, *The Act of Marriage*, (Toronto: Bantam Books, 1984), p. 133.

[5] Ibid., p. 33.

view on her role as a woman, wife, and possible mother. She said, "After I have grown old, shall I have pleasure, my lord, being old also?" Sarah acknowledged with this brief introspection that the sexual relationship brought physical pleasure. She loved her husband, Abraham, and by their story we know that he loved her deeply. She longed to give him a child, but could not. This Bible couple shared an intimacy that thousands of barren couples share. With hearts broken for the lack of a child, they had each other with which to share their feelings. Old age of the couple did not change the closeness of the two though the strength of their passions had lessened with time. This again reminds us that intimacy does not always involve the sexual act.

Their son Isaac grew up with two loving parents who taught him, by example, what intimacy was all about. He grew up knowing that intimacy was a vital part of keeping a relationship alive and well. When he and Rebekah traveled to Gerar, they came to King Abimelech, ruler of the Philistines. Like his father before him, Isaac lied to the king, telling him that Rebekah was his sister instead of his wife. God did not have to intervene as he did in Abraham's situation. After Isaac and Rebekah had been in Gerar a long while, Abimelech spotted "Isaac showing endearment to Rebekah his wife" (Gen. 26:1-8). This clearly reflects the love and physical desire and the attraction that they had for one another. The King James Version uses the term *sporting*. This term in the Hebrew language is *tsachaq* which means "to sport, play, toy with, of conjugal caresses."[6] The NIV uses the term *caressing* while the NKJV employs the words *showing endearment*. By the attention Isaac was giving Rebekah, even this heathen king knew that what he was seeing was more than just sibling affection. He easily recognized two people in love. The separation the two endured in Gerar caused them both to be eager for the

[6] Francis Brown, S. R. Driver, and C. A. Briggs, *Hebrew and English Lexicon of the Old Testament,* (Oxford: Clarendon Press), p. 850.

other's touch. Isaac needed his wife and Rebekah needed her husband. Though the Bible doesn't say that Rebekah did any sporting, her acceptance of it affirmed the king's suspicion that brother and sister they were not.

Solomon helped us to understand the nature of love and being in love in the book of Song of Solomon. He captivates the reader with the love story between the Shulamite maiden and himself. This candid portrayal reveals passionate kisses, embraces, and love words so clearly spoken that neither the maiden nor the king could misunderstand their message. King Solomon fell in love with this woman and wooed her. He chased her and pursued her, finally winning her hand in marriage. He constantly assured her of his love and adoration. The maiden also was full of romance. She wished to be close to her love as often as possible. She shared her feelings and thoughts about her fiancé with the daughters of Jerusalem. She also never failed to let the king himself know her admiration of him and her physical attraction and desire for him. This book clearly relates to the reader that tender passion should never be allowed to flicker out and die. When was the last time you told your husband how you feel about him? Go on, make the first move. Let him know how special he is.

Another woman who was not at all timid with showing her husband that she was attracted to him and interested in him was the virtuous woman in Proverbs 31. There are only two verses that mention her husband but they speak volumes about her. In verse 23 he is mentioned as being known at the city gates and sitting with the elders of the land, and in verse 28 he is mentioned because he calls his wife blessed and he praises her. Intimacy begins long before touching or physical closeness develops. Before they have intimacy, a couple must have mutual interests. There must be conversation. Intimacy requires respect, self-control, unselfishness, love and concern for others, kindness, and a conscious effort to always act in the best interest of the one you love. The woman mentioned in Proverbs 31 portrayed all of these qualities. And the simple reason we know this is because her husband praised her. How many husbands that do not experience a richly intimate relationship praise their wives publicly? This is a good sign of a happily satisfied and deeply loved man.

Proverbs 5:3-19 is another frank passage about the sexual intimacies in marriage. Wise Solomon, knowing the strong inclinations of man, gives sound instructions for the young man. He specifically encourages the man who might be drawn toward an adulterous affair to "drink water from your own cistern" (v. 15). The man needs to be faithful and true as does the woman. Solomon tells the husband that his wife is to be his own and not to be shared with other men. He is to rejoice with the wife of his youth and is to be happy with her alone (v. 18). As is stated in the New Testament, a wife's body is not her own but belongs to her husband (1 Cor. 7:4). Solomon knew this to be true when he said "Let her breasts satisfy you at all times. And always be enraptured with her love" (Prov. 5:19). The love and commitment that a woman gives her husband is more satisfying and fulfilling than the short-term sexual gratification offered by an adulterous affair with an immoral woman. Sadly we sometimes see that the wife of a man is simply not willing to allow sexual intimacy or any other type of closeness, for that matter. Plainly and simply put, this is a sin. The woman has a God-given obligation to fulfill her role as a wife if she is married. If she does not have a change of heart by making her marriage all it can be, she is disobeying God and will be accountable for her lack of love for her husband.

To be intimate one must understand that one's speech has much to do with how close another wishes to be. A husband once told me that it was very undesirable to cuddle a hissing snake. By this he meant that he did not feel very close to his wife at times when all she did was snap and snarl at him for little things. Do we pay attention to the tone of voice we use with our husbands? Do we grumble and gripe about every little thing (Prov. 21:9, 19)? Do we nag him needlessly? Be honest now! Are we guilty of goading him and picking fights (Prov. 26:21)? Do we answer him with a quick sharp tone or with a soft, kind answer (Prov. 15:1)? Are we often bossy, speaking to him as we would to a child? Do we try to humiliate or embarrass him in public (Prov. 11:22; 12:4)? Do we attempt to bulldoze our husbands into submission when it is we who should be submitting? Do we allow intimacy to be present by submitting to his leadership in our home? Remember the old saying, "A woman is the only creature that can conquer by submitting."

Sexual intimacy, as a couple ages, can slow down considerably and sometimes come to a halt altogether. Because of slow and subtle physical, psychological, and hormonal changes, we may notice that we have very little physical contact with our mate. For women, menopause can be the culprit. As the female hormones decrease, so does her sex drive. Due to this hormonal decrease, her body does not produce the lubrication it once did and therefore what used to be pleasurable can be uncomfortable or even painful. She may think that her husband is no longer as gentle as he once was and may resist his advances. And, of course, with no communication, he may feel as if she is no longer interested in him sexually.[7] With medical advances we now have the opportunity to seek help from trusted doctors. Discuss your problems openly and ask for their help.

Men do not escape physical changes brought about by age. Testosterone levels decrease in males after the age of thirty. Their sexual drive declines but this does not necessarily mean that their pleasure is decreased. As a man and woman begin to notice changes in their sex life, they can work together to continue to make their love life as rewarding as it has always been.

[7] Edwin Kiester, Jr. and Sally Valente Kiester, "Sex after Thirty," *Reader's Digest,* (Pleasantville, NY: Reader's Digest Association, Inc., 1995), November, 1995, p. 11.

Adjustments may be needed and this takes communication on the part of both partners. Take time with each other. Don't rush things. As the husband and wife age together the sexual timing becomes closer. The man's excitement is brought about at a slower rate than when he was younger and so more closely matches that of his spouse. After thirty-five, he may be turned on less by what he sees than by his wife's kissing and caressing.

> "Once a couple learns to pay less attention to what they see and more to what they do," says New York sex and marital therapist Shirley Zussman, "their sex lives improve dramatically."[8]

It is a known fact that men and women alike produce testosterone and estrogen. But the levels of these hormones change as time passes. The male's testosterone decreases and the estrogen level rises while the female's estrogen level decreases and the testosterone level increases. This may cause the woman to be more sexually assertive while the husband may be content to enjoy this transposition, enjoying a slightly more passive role.

Be aware that with age comes changes. Acknowledgment encourages adjustment. Realize that intercourse is not all there is to sexual satisfaction. Treasure each special moment of closeness and realize that two can still be one if they put less emphasis on how often but rather emphasize how intimate their oneness is.

Each woman will make her choice. If intimacy in your marriage is not what you want it to be, it is in yours and your husband's power to change it. It takes a conscious effort and some attitude adjustments to achieve a long-lasting change in one's life. But with a renewed commitment to God and to each other, you can attain your goal to have a marriage that brings a little heaven to earth.

---

[8] Ibid., p. 14.

5

The Two Shall Become One, But . . .

LeAnn Duke

Most young women grow up with the God-designed expectation and desire to find that special someone with whom to spend their life. When God designed man, He knew that only woman could sufficiently meet man's needs. This was in God's plan from creation. God gave man a helper meet or fit for him. Solomon wrote in Proverbs 18:22 that "he who finds a wife finds a good thing."

But the Bible shows that marriage is not for everyone. God commanded Jeremiah not to marry because of the future battles that would take the lives of many of God's chosen people, including a wife and any children that would be born to Jeremiah (Jer. 16:1-4). Paul chose not to marry and, because of the "present distress," urged those who were unmarried to remain single so that they could dedicate their lives to the work of the kingdom (1 Cor. 7:26-33). God's plan for man included a wife who would complete him. With the presentation of woman, Adam declared, "Therefore a man shall leave his father and mother and be joined to his wife, and they shall become one flesh" (Gen. 2:24). But . . .

The Two May Never Meet

"Do you have someone special in your life?" or "Do you have a boyfriend?" or even more insensitive "You're not married yet?" are common questions asked to those past eighteen and single. The unrelenting pressure placed on young women today to be in a hurry to find a boyfriend is appalling. I have been shocked to find that many mothers and fathers think it is "cute" that their twelve or thirteen-year-old daughters are actually dating. The puppy love that many young girls experience is soon accelerated by over-anxious parents into something far more serious than young emotions can handle. Some fear that their daughters might never marry, so they overcompensate by nudging their blossoming daughters who are still children into situations that they are not able to handle. That is only one of the reasons for the overwhelming rate of teen pregnancy.

The young single woman contemplates what sort of man will be in her future. She may worry at times whether there will be a man in her future. She may even wonder at times if she is being "too picky." Well meaning friends and relatives can unknowingly put the wrong kind of pressure on a conscientious young woman by rushing her to find a mate. There are many difficult questions to ask as she goes through this period in her life. Relationships may come and go and she may remain single. But the ultimate goal of the single woman wishing to marry should never be to lower her standards in her search for a Christian husband. Any young person who is committed to finding a mate with the same views on marriage should be congratulated and admired instead of being criticized.

But let us discuss two different classes of single women. Marriage is God-ordained but may not be for everyone. What about the young woman who is single by choice? This person is perfectly normal. The apostle Paul was a single man (1 Cor. 7:7). He very likely chose to remain this way because of his lifestyle. He seemed content and even wished that others could remain as he. There is nothing unnatural about the woman who prefers to remain single and take care of only herself. As a Christian woman, she can have a wonderful life of service, caring for those in need of help. She can devote hours to lifting the weak-spirited, caring for the sick, helping the elderly, visiting the bereaved, and performing many other acts of kindness that married women find difficult to perform because their time is already spread thin by caring for the needs of their families (1 Cor. 7:32-33). The single woman has the option of choosing a career which allows her freedom to do special acts. Opportunities may arise in which a single woman can arrange her work schedule so she can travel on mission trips to help teach women and children in a foreign field. Mission work gives a special sense of fulfillment.

The second class is the woman who strongly desires to marry but may never be able to find the suitable mate. She may not lack for male friends and may have a strong attraction for one or two of them, but the feelings may not be returned. She may develop only brotherly affection with her male friends. She might repeatedly be asked to go to dinner, a movie, or a party, but the relationship either stays a "buddy" kind of friendship or the guy never calls back. She may not be totally satisfied with her situation. She may dream of marriage and desire a family. She just doesn't seem to meet anyone who returns her interest in pursuing a relationship. So what is wrong with her? Why can't she find the quality of man she wants? Why doesn't the one she wants to be with want to be with her?

First of all, nothing is wrong with her. She can be proud of the standards she has set for herself. It is hard for any of us to understand where her future lies. But the young woman who finds herself alone should look to God for guidance and not burden herself with recriminations or self-pity. This can be very damaging. The less confidence one has in herself, the less confidence and interest another will have in her. Sadly, this is not a society that allows people to be comfortable with themselves if they are alone. But a single man or woman can be a complete and whole person. To choose to be single doesn't mean that one is selfish or wrong in some way. God made each person different. If you cannot seem to find the right mate, look at the reasons you want to be married. Are you looking for financial security or a way out of a difficult situation? Are you searching for a legitimate reason for sexual fulfillment or a way to have a child? Are you searching for the right kind of face or the right kind of body? If so, all of the above reasons can and most likely will lead a girl to wish she had remained single. Again, attitude is the primary focus in any kind of lifestyle. Whether the single life is chosen or beyond one's control, the way we look at ourselves will result in what we become as we grow older.

Being single can bring some matters of concern. One of those is loneliness. Questions are posed to the unmarried: "Aren't you ever lonely?" "Do you enjoy eating alone?" "You go to the theater alone?" "Isn't it difficult to fix a meal for just one?" Depending on the person's attitude the answers will vary. Does the single woman get lonely? Of course she does. She is a God-created being and has needs and feelings. She desires to be close to others and to develop and cultivate friendships. The difference is her attitude, her priorities, her commitment to herself. When a single woman gets lonely, what does she do about it? Does she sit and sulk, feel sorry for herself, or get angry? The choice is rather a simple one. Her responsibilities are for herself alone so this allows her to be more flexible than the woman who attempts to maintain her schedule, her husband's schedule, the children's schedule, church obligations, club meetings, and PTO meetings. She can call a friend, entertain friends at home, arrange shopping trips with the young teen girls at her congregation, or visit a widowed or single member of the congregation who is probably more lonely than she. Getting out and doing for someone else whose need is greater than one's own is a cure for the blues. The single life of a Christian can be as full as one likes, or it can be as empty and lonely as one allows. The opportunities of the single woman are numerous. The perspective one has of her life can result in a serene, peaceful, and satisfying future.

Another concern is the matter of sexual desire for the single woman. How does the single woman handle remaining sexually pure? Does the single woman have as strong a desire as the married woman? What if the woman dates often and is attracted to a man who is not attracted to her for the right reasons? Does she feel tempted to give in to sex for fear of never fulfilling bodily desires?

From the pre-teen years, the hormonal balance in the woman's body shifts and changes, bringing on moods, emotional upheavals, and responses that leave us breathless and shocked at their intensity. She must deal with blue times, moodiness, irritability, and desire, and the single woman is not immune. The body experiences these sensations, but one thing should be emphasized: Sexual desire is a state of mind and not just a bodily sensation. Sexual purity begins in the mind. "For as he thinks in his heart, so is he" (Prov. 23:7). What we allow our minds to dwell on is what we will eventually allow to become a part of our lives. What we watch on television, read in books, look at in magazines, listen to on the radio, and talk about with our friends can soon change the way we think. Don't be fooled! These choices do affect us. The devil tries to stimulate our worldly appetites by desensitizing us. He slowly but consistently projects evil as good to the point that our conscience is dulled. What once offended us no longer bothers us. We must be on guard against Satan at all times. Sometimes our greatest desire can be used to hurt us.

The Bible teaches that sexual desire is to be fulfilled by those who are married and that those who participate in this sexual union are acceptable in God's sight (Heb. 13:4). Those, however, who participate in this union who are not married are committing sin before God (Deut. 22:22; Matt. 19:9). Sexual purity is important and should be taught, encouraged, and deeply ingrained in young men and women from childhood on through their adult life. Paul told the people at Corinth that his wish was that "all men were even as I myself" (1 Cor. 7:7). In verse 7 he also gives a reason why some could remain single: "But each one has his own gift from God, one in this manner and another in that." Some may have less sexual desire than others and may be able to control their desire better than others. In verse 8 he urges the widows and the unmarried to remain single as he was if they could exercise self-control. No matter what the physical urge is or how strong it is, God expects us to maintain control over our bodily appetites. One may say, "Oh sure, you can say that, you're married," or "You just don't know how he makes me feel." Of course we do. Sexual desires were made by God to be strong enough to bring man and woman together in order to procreate. But that was not the only reason that God gave man the natural desire for sex. It was to fulfill man, to satisfy him, to bring happiness to him. But human beings still have the free will and the ability to control what they do.

A man who encourages a young woman to engage in fondling or sexual intercourse by telling her that he "loves her" does *not* love her. He has lust in his heart for her, but he does not love her. The man who uses this kind of deception certainly has no respect for her. Most who have been promiscuous will admit that they quickly lost respect for the person they were intimate with. They soon found they had nothing in common and did not even like one another. Their sexual fulfillment was not complete because there was a stronger feeling to combat: guilt.

The young woman who uses her body to entice men to lust is guilty of the same lack of respect. She may use her sexuality to control her male friends and this is just as wrong. God will hold her accountable for her actions. The simple fact is that God gave men as well as women the capacity for self-control. And though sexual desire is the second strongest human appetite, it can be managed. Each one of us has the responsibility to gain control over our own lusts, whether they be for food, drink, or sex. God expects us to exercise self-control.

Our future is ultimately in God's hands though we often attempt to depend on ourselves. We sometimes fail to remember to ask God for His providential care. For the single woman searching for a mate, be sure to work on your inner self and become the person God wants you to be. Study God's Word and let it be your guide. Be satisfied at the stage in which you find yourself, but always strive to reach your goal. Be ready to accept God's answers to your prayers, realizing they may not be in line with what you expected. Don't be afraid to pray and be specific. The following requests will get you started:

- Pray to God, daily asking Him to help you become the person He wants you to be.

- Pray that God will help you to find the best mate for you.

- Pray that God will help you and your future mate be ready for marriage at the same time.

- Then relax and enjoy your life and let things happen in God's time. God's way is best.

Death Separates the Two—Widowhood

"I take this man to be my husband, to live with him through good times and bad, in sickness and health, till death . . ." The excitement of the day, the depth of love shared between the bride and groom, and the dreams of a future together can cloud reality and blur the future. Realistically, one of the two will die, leaving the other alone.

It happened to me. In November of 1979, I married my best friend. I had not known him long, but I found in him the Christian qualities for which I had searched. We married at twenty-two and moved back to his home town in Kentucky. I was content to begin my new life as a loving

wife and to start a family with him. We bought our first
home in 1983, the same year that our first child was born.
Our second child was born a year-and-a-half later and we
felt our life was complete. Our love had grown in the years
we were blessed to be together.

My entire world was shattered on July 21, 1989. Brian
went to work as usual. But that was the only normal thing
about that day. He died in an auto accident within an hour
after leaving home. The secure married life I had known a
short time before was now gone. I was a widow and a single
mother of two children. I worked part-time and now was
totally responsible for taking care of our family. The shock
was enormous. I could not envision my life without Brian
in it. As I tried to take in what had happened, my mind
was in a whirl. I wanted to deny the truth. When I first
learned of Brian's death I told myself that it was a mistake, a case of mistaken identification. Guiltily, I now am
able to admit that I hoped it was someone else's husband.
I felt that if something had happened, I would surely have
known it. I was his wife and I would have sensed if he was
hurt—or dead. But I had sensed or felt nothing. I was taken
to the hospital by a close friend for what I thought would
be confirmation of his identity. I was left in a small office
alone for several minutes. I prayed and begged God not to
let it be true. I prayed that Brian would just walk through
the door and tell me it had all been just a terrible mistake.
The sheriff and the coroner entered and I was given Brian's
personal belongings and they offered their sincere condo-
lence for my loss. My husband was gone and I was truly
alone for the first time in almost ten years—more alone
than before I married.

It is difficult to determine what emotions one feels when
tragedy strikes so suddenly. I recall the anger being so
strong that it frightened me. I was shocked that I hurt so
much and could be so angry at the same time. I was angry
because of the unfairness. I was angry at the negligence of
the driver of the truck who struck Brian's truck head-on.

The shocking thing to me was that I was also angry with Brian for leaving me alone to make all the decisions, for leaving me to raise our son and daughter alone, and to take care of the responsibilities of life by myself. The burden was enormous and I did not feel I was able to handle it. I was frightened at making the wrong decisions. I thought I knew so much about life until I faced being accountable for everything. I soon found out how blissfully ignorant I had been. Of course I knew that we had life insurance, but I never thought it would be me contacting the company. I didn't even know the name of the company. A few years before, we had the foresight to see an attorney and make out our wills, but I thought we would be eighty or ninety years old before we needed them. The paperwork facing me was enormous and I was in no frame of mind to deal with that burden, but I had no choice. Decisions had to be made whether I was ready or not. I filled out the necessary forms for Brian's life insurance and contacted the necessary companies. I was fortunate that Brian's will did not have to go through probate, though in the state in which we lived, I was notified that I had to be made legal guardian of my own children. There are only a few things that can be done to lessen the paperwork when a spouse dies. Having a will takes an enormous burden off the spouse remaining.

Along with the anger came fear. I was scared of doing the wrong thing and did not want others to see that I was afraid. I learned that with grief many times one feeling is present to hide another. Anger would mask the fear and I would often have trouble distinguishing the two feelings. Remember that these emotions are normal and they are beneficial in their own way to help one to deal with the reality of the loss.

As the anger subsided another emotion crashed in on me. Being angry with Brian for dying brought about extreme guilt because I knew he was blameless. I felt so selfish. I knew it was not his choice to die that day. But guilt is present and one needs to understand that it is a feeling that, if ignored, can delay recovery. I remember a different kind of guilt. I often asked the question, "Why not me?" because I wished that I had died too. Why did it have to be him? I felt guilty for being the one to survive, to see our children grow up and do all the things we had looked forward to seeing them do together. When I felt really rotten I asked God, "Why did this happen to me? Why could it have not been someone else?" I was jolted out of my self pity by other questions: "Why not me?" "Why should this happen to anyone else?" "Why should I be exempt?" Would I really want someone to experience this kind of pain? I have learned to be careful about taking life for granted.

Death strikes every family, each individual (Heb. 9:27). There is no stopping it. The only control we have is to be prepared spiritually to die. We can control some things in our physical life, too. Make a will. It can be done with an attorney or in some states something as simple as a video-tape telling your family your desires in the event of your death. In the event of a terminal illness, a living will needs to be drawn up, signed, and notarized. This can also be done for those who want to have their wishes known in the event of an accident leaving them incapacitated. Discuss these things with your mate and learn his desires should his life be taken suddenly. Don't be afraid to discuss death. We openly discuss our plans for tomorrow or next week. But often we fear speaking of death to a loved one. It is frightening and unpleasant to actually make plans for one's life after one's mate is gone. It definitely does not seem real even when some see death coming, such as with a terminal illness. Talk to them about their wishes: who is to speak at their funeral, where they wish to be buried, what kind of casket they want, and who their pallbearers will be. Funeral arrangements are really no different than selecting health or life insurance. If the funeral homes in your city offer prearranged plans, check into them. Doing so relieves an enormous burden for the remaining spouse.

It shows great love and concern for your spouse and you can know that when the time comes, those difficult arrangements will not be a burden to your spouse.

Learning to deal with my widowhood was the next step. I felt like a baby learning to walk. I would do well one day and fall apart the next. Out of nowhere anger or guilt would surface and I'd begin the healing process all over again. I got discouraged and felt like giving up. But I knew I couldn't because I had two children for which I was responsible. And I knew that God would give me strength to keep going. The emotions of grief can be overwhelming and it can seem the end is nowhere in sight. However, when it was pointed out to me that all these feelings are a natural part of grief, it became much easier to deal with them. I was no longer afraid to let myself experience them. It was a good release. Did it make it any easier to be without my husband? No. But I was no longer afraid of the obscure and disturbing feelings that made me worry about my sanity.

Understanding the different emotions that make up grief helps one to handle whatever may come. Acknowledging the feelings for what they really are is the first step to being able to handle the emotional upheavals that will come. Tears are a normal part of grief. We should not be afraid or embarrassed to cry. Many feel guilty for crying so much and others feel guilty for not crying enough. Tears are God's way for us to cleanse the pain and sorrow from our hearts and help to heal us physically and emotionally. Many are afraid to empty themselves because those feelings frighten them. I can remember crying and being frightened by the sounds that came from me. I had never loved or hurt so deeply before. The surviving spouse should not feel guilty about being a survivor. I don't know why my husband died that day but I know that since then I have grown in ways that I would never have if death had not struck our home. Tragedy and hardships can help individuals to grow. They can turn one from worldly living to seeking a more godly life. I still grieve at times for Brian.

He will never be forgotten. The grief has greatly lessened with time, but I still miss him and am sad at times that he is no longer physically in my life. But I thank God daily for his short presence in my life because I learned a great deal about myself from him. He taught me many great lessons that enabled me to have confidence in myself to deal with many difficult situations. Through widowhood I learned that God's way is not man's way: "It is not in man that walketh to direct his steps" (Jer. 10:23).

How long should a widow grieve? How long should she wait before she dates or remarries? There is no scripturally designated time for mourning. Each individual's needs are different. Also the length of their mourning varies from culture to culture. A widow should be allowed to decide for herself when it is time to move forward in her life. She does not forget the person or the loss. One should be able to come to friends for advice, but one's friendship should not be hinged upon whether she takes that advice or decides to begin dating or remarry. The widow will undoubtedly feel her own guilt about the changes taking place in her life. The man she thought she would spend the rest of her life with is no longer there. She may feel guilty for having a good time with friends, especially a new male friend. She will likely feel a certain disloyalty to her deceased husband's memory or may even feel as if she has been unfaithful. This is normal. But nowhere in the Scriptures is a woman confined to a life of solitude because she is widowed. In fact, the Bible tells us just the opposite: "A wife is bound by law as long as her husband lives; but if her husband dies, she is at liberty to be married to whom she wishes, only in the Lord" (1 Cor. 7:39). The time one remains single is strictly a matter of choice. The problem begins when family members, friends, or acquaintances question the widow's decision to date when she has the right to do so. Paul urged the younger widows to remarry (1 Tim. 5:14) for the sake of their God-given sexual desire.

If there had been a decreed time limit for widows to remain widows, Paul would have surely mentioned this.

It is common for those who have had happy marriages to seek remarriage much sooner than those who were in a strained or unhappy union. In general, though, it may be wise to make no major decisions from one to two years after the death of a spouse due to the extreme emotional upheaval. Regret for the sale of a home or a hasty remarriage can cause a great deal of guilt, pain, and sadness. But the length of time in which the person waits is ultimately up to the individual.

Grief is a process, a passage from one of life's circumstances to another. It is a slower journey for some than for others. As death visits each of us, we must understand that it too is a passage into another life. Though we will be changed in body, our souls will be the same. Instead of fearing and avoiding this subject, we should ready ourselves and our loved ones. Prepare for tomorrow, though we do not have assurance of tomorrow. James asks us, "For what is your life? It is even a vapor that appears for a little time and then vanishes away" (James 4:14). If one has followed the biblical examples for salvation, then death is not to be feared. Dread and sadness in leaving loved ones is always present but there should be confidence for the faithful Christian who faces death.

The Two May Divorce

Divorce continues to ravage our society, invade our homes, and destroy and separate our families. And it is not just happening to the proverbial Joneses anymore. It strikes more and more Christian homes. Preachers, elders, deacons, and the most highly respected Christian men and women are leaving their spouses. Generally speaking, most have become apathetic towards God's Word in regards to marriage, divorce, and remarriage. It ultimately comes down to a total lack of respect for God's Word. When men and women truly love and respect God's Word, they will strive to keep His will. Their own desires will automatically come second.

Like death, divorce brings a devastating impact. The emotions brought by divorce are very similar to those of death; however, there are significant differences. Grief comes wrapped in different packages and no one feeling is to be counted as abnormal. Anger, guilt, fear, and inadequacy are only a few of these feelings.

Intense anger is perhaps a misunderstood sentiment caused by divorce. Many well-meaning friends might say, "Anger will only hurt you. Put it aside and get on with your life." If only it were that simple. The Bible justifies righteous anger (Mark 3:5). And one's anger is completely justified when her spouse has violated her trust and the intimacy of their oneness by having an affair. It is perfectly natural, and if you are not angry, then you are either not being honest with yourself or there is a deeper problem. Anger can provoke sinful actions so one must be in control (Eph. 4:26). Facing the one who betrays you in a gentle way is usually neither realistic nor advisable. A Christian should always act Christ-like though, keeping in mind that Christ displayed His feelings. It is not sinful to show distaste for the sin of the guilty, nor is it sinful to let the person know you do not uphold or condone his sin. Hate, however, is a sin, though many who have been through a divorce due to the fornication of their mate admit that it is most difficult to avoid. But we should not allow ourselves to stay angry because we know that it is destructive. Allowing rage to control your life will eventually affect relationships that you desire to keep. It can harm your work relationships, your friendships, and even your relationship with your children. Anger promotes bitterness and your soul will be in jeopardy.

How do you deal with the anger? First, admit that it is present. Second, acknowledge your right to feel it and then deal with it, not allowing yourself to give in to the temptation to sin.

When a marriage ends, guilt will likely come crashing in on the innocent party as well as the guilty. You may think, "I have no reason to feel guilty." But the emotion is present anyway. You may find yourself reviewing the past to see if you did something that could account for your spouse's departure. You may "beat yourself over the head" for past mistakes. Although the Bible teaches that an individual should do a regular checkup of one's life (2 Cor. 13:5), it does not teach us to take responsibility for another's sin. Ask the questions: Were you faithful to him? Did you love him as God expects a wife to love her husband? Were you submissive as God would have you to be? Did you do all you could do to make your marriage work? Was your husband guilty of fornication? Did he betray your vows? If so, then your guilt is not valid. Everyone makes mistakes. No one is agreeable all the time. No one is in perfect control at all times. Errors are expected but there is never an excuse for an individual to commit fornication. You can recount the past and examine your motives for decisions made. If the facts are still the same, then guilt for the divorce has no place in your life. It may be that children are involved and you may feel guilty for their sakes, especially if you are the one seeking the dissolution of the marriage. They may place blame on you for not allowing their father to return home. This can be devastating and there is no easy way to deal with their unhappiness or anger at a situation beyond their control.

Love, patience, time, and consistent Bible teaching will eventually help to ease the tension of the situation. Many children find it difficult to be angry with the guilty parent and they choose to ignore the blatant fact of sin. Realize though that they carry with them some of the same feelings you do: hurt, rejection, guilt, anger, and feelings of being unlovable. They just show them in different ways.

However, we must also realize that as our children grow up, they will make a conscious choice of how they wish to deal with the infidelity of the unfaithful parent. They may choose to completely ignore the betrayal, blaming the innocent party instead. They may choose to lead a lifestyle somewhat similar to the guilty parent. This too is beyond your control. It is very painful but being prepared helps to deal with the emotional strain. This is why it is so vital to teach your children what God says about the importance and the purity of marriage. Sadly though, because free will enters the picture, children sometimes do not make the right choice. After the divorce, the everyday dealings with your children will likely present more of a burden than you ever imagined. Your response to them can vary from paying too little attention to them and not giving enough discipline, to going overboard and lashing out at them for the most minor offenses. You may also find yourself lavishing them with treats and gifts that you cannot afford because you feel responsible for their melancholy moods. This can be especially true if you are the one seeking the divorce and have custody of the children. Remember that being open and honest with the children without being bitter and hateful is vital. They need to know that God's love for them has not changed. Yours and their father's love for them is still the same. But due to a selfish decision, there are consequences that everyone must endure.

Shame is another stigma of divorce. You feel your marriage was a sham and you are now another statistic. How do you face your family and friends? Will they think of you as a failure? You may wonder if you will be stigmatized for the rest of your life. Like a widow, you are now left single in a world that seemingly is only comfortable with couples. It may seem easier to withdraw. But be careful and realize that during this time you need your friends and family more than ever. Your church family can be invaluable, but do not let your shame and bitterness allow you to resent them because they are a little uncomfortable and do not seem to know what to do or say. If they ask you if they can help you, express your thanks and then let them help. If you are having financial trouble and someone offers to help, let them. If they offer to spend time with you, though you may feel like pulling back, take them up on it. Someone may offer to keep your kids for you one night to let you have a break. If this happens, let them do it for you without feeling guilty. You need the time to yourself and your kids probably need time away from you. You cannot be a good mother if you are worn to a frazzle. Being a single mother with no one to relieve you can make you resentful. Your children will be the first ones to suffer. Keep in mind they need you now more than ever. Don't be afraid to give yourself a break. You will be surprised at how refreshed you feel with just one night to yourself.

A betrayed person may experience the feeling of being unlovable or undesirable. This insecurity is especially strong in women. She feels that if her husband chose another woman that there must be something wrong with her. This is not at all true. The lovableness of a person is not dependent on the actions of another. Each individual has a right to expect that she is endearing to another, especially her husband. She may not be a physical beauty but that does not make her unlovable. She may be fat or skinny, tall or short, plain or pretty, but she is made in the image of God and is therefore a beautiful creature and in every way worthy of love. The spouse who feels that he has the right to cast aside the vows promised before God and selfishly seek an intimate relationship with another forfeits his right to have a life of fulfilling and satisfying love.

A reaction to divorce that is normally not present with death is failure. You want to vent your anger, cry the tears of sadness, rage, disappointment, hate, frustration, loneliness, and even desire. Daily you may feel some or all of these. You may want to lay down somewhere and give up, but you know that you must carry on, handling life and the blows it has dealt. The grief you experience will at times make you think you are losing touch with the real world. You no longer have interest in the same things you once did. You may not be able to think straight. Details get jumbled and you seem to be intolerant of even the most simple mistake. You cannot seem to rest at night; you feel tired all day. Your energy level is zero. You find that your every breath turns into dispirited sighs. You are gripped by heartbreaking grief. You are in mourning. For a Christian woman who married a Christian man this is especially true. She may wonder what difference it makes in choosing a Christian over a non-Christian.

A woman whose marriage has dissolved may wonder what she is to do about the sexual desire she still strongly feels. Separation and divorce do not normally cause one to stop feeling. A woman may still love her husband, though she knows she cannot trust him. She may still crave his attention. Though divorced, she still has the need to be held and touched, and to hear tender, loving words. The desire for sexual intimacy does not go away. She may experience familiar strong feelings of desire toward the very one who has betrayed her, only to be followed by anger and repulsion toward the betrayer.

Fear is a very strong emotion for a divorced woman. She fears being on her own, because she has always relied on her husband. If she has children she may receive no monetary support from him and find that she is now the sole provider. She may have to look for work or get a second job to take care of her children. Being afraid does not just hinge on the financial arrangements of a family now fatherless and husbandless. Her self-esteem is quite possibly low and she may also fear someone will take advantage of her. These feelings do not go away quickly. It takes time to heal and to gain confidence. Some scars are very deep and for many women it takes much longer. But the memories of good times, bad times, loving times, and angry times challenge her to grow in spite of the pain.

The Bible is specific when dealing with the subject of fornication. It declares only one reason for divorce, that of fornication or sexual immorality. In Matthew 19:9 Jesus clearly described the legitimate motive for the dividing of what God has joined together. "And I say unto you, Whoever divorces his wife, except for sexual immorality and marries another commits adultery; and whoever marries her who is divorced commits adultery" (NKJV). Notice the phrase "except for sexual immorality." In Greek the word *except* literally means "if not" (*ei me*). It is really a very simple passage to understand. *Except* means "on any other condition than, unless."[9] So unless a husband has been sexually unfaithful to his wife, she cannot obtain a divorce from him with God's approval. This applies to those inside the church and those outside the church. Divorce is not legitimate on the grounds that a wife is not a faithful Christian, a husband drinks, or a wife wastes money. It cannot be biblically condoned if a husband or wife does not fulfil his/her conjugal obligation. One's mate being nasty tempered or a nag does not give the wife God's authorization for putting him away. Fornication is the only reason (Matt. 5:32; 19:9).

Divorce is like death in that it is a journey from one kind of life to another. The changes in one's perspective that are brought about by divorce are a matter of one's choosing. Overcoming calamity or being destroyed by it are a matter of will. One can be divorced and still be a faithful Christian if the desire to please God remains a priority.

The Two May Become His, Mine, and Ours

Stepfamilies have become much more prevalent in this age. However, they are not a new phenomenon. Over the last decade the divorce and remarriage rate has sharply increased and the remarriages of young and older widows

[9] *Webster's Ninth New Collegiate Dictionary,* (Springfield, MA: Merriam-Webster Inc., 1991), p. 432.

have produced stepfamilies or what are more popularly called blended families. The Bible has many such portrayals: Keturah, Abraham's second wife was Isaac's stepmother; two of Jacob's children, Joseph and Benjamin, had Leah for a stepmother; Moses' children possibly had a stepmother when he took the Ethiopian woman as his wife; and anyone who married a widower with children would step into the role of stepmother.

The first consideration for any woman who is considering becoming a stepmother, or who has already become a stepmother, is the natural affection of a child toward his mother. This is very important. The Bible speaks of this feeling in 2 Timothy 3:3. Do not underestimate the natural love between a mother and her children. Though you may enter into a relationship with no intentions of trying to take the place of the child's mother, it can happen very easily, especially if the children's father has custodial rights. You will see the child daily. In practice, you will become the mother to the stepchild that you are to your own children.

When one enters the "step" relationship with a child, it is precarious at best. This is especially true if the child is old enough to understand who his biological mother is and if the mother is in close proximity to the child and has visiting rights. While you may think only of helping the child to deal with the divorce of his parents, the child may secretly harbor resentment or even a full-blown hatred of you. You may be viewed as an intruder in the home or an enemy of the child. He may blame you for his mother and father's divorce, though he knows deep down that it is not true. The child may clearly see that you love his father deeply and that you love him too, but anger and disappointment at his parents keep him antagonistic. You must also be prepared for the possibility of jealousy on the part of the natural mother. She may be jealous because you are with her former husband, though she chose to break the vow and commit fornication. She may take an immediate dislike to you only because you are with her child and she is not. She may have given custody of the child to the father, wanting no responsibilities where the child is concerned. The love she feels for her child nowhere matches the desire to please herself. The motive behind her jealousy could be guilt for leaving the child in the first place. Very few mothers feel pleasure in seeing their child respond in love toward a woman they view as their rival, even if they are guilty and made the choice to leave the child behind.

Be realistic when assessing the depth of the relationship that you can build with the child. Be willing to acknowledge that the child's first loyalty will, in most cases, be to his mother, not to you. He could very well love you and respond to you in a positive way. But if his mother sees him on a regular basis, be prepared for the child to be apprehensive about his relationship with you. He may not allow himself to freely give his love to you (though he may wish to) because he feels disloyal to his natural mother. The mother usually sees, or at least senses, the closeness developing. She may use the child's natural affection toward her for her own gain. She may make the child feel incredibly guilty for depending on or loving another besides herself. She may kindle the child's mistrust or dislike of you by telling falsehoods.

Stepfamilies are more complicated when they involve a Christian home and a non-Christian home. As the child readies himself for visits to his mother's home, he is leaving a Christian environment for a non-Christian environment. He may be apprehensive and nervous. Though he wants to see his mother, he may not know what to expect when he is with her. What kinds of things will he witness? If the mother of the child was guilty of immorality, she may still be actively pursuing this lifestyle. Will she be promiscuous in the child's presence? With what kind of people will she be spending her time? What kind of example will she/they be setting for the child? Will he be safe?

Will he go to worship services? What kind of entertainment (movies, activities) will she allow him to enjoy? Will she be drinking? Will there be drugs in the house? Will she even have time for her child? Remember that the child will have an equally hard time adjusting to a woman whom he now only sees occasionally. He will have to adjust to things now that he likely has never seen before. The situations from one household to another change so rapidly the child is confused and scared. But his need to be with his mother is so great he will endure almost any situation to be able to see her, hug her, kiss her, or spend even a few hours with her, though real danger may be present. Realize that when the child arrives home, his disposition may be entirely different from when he left. He may appear distant, sad, angry, or may revert to unacceptable behavior. This is common. The child is stuck in the middle of a bad situation precipitated by adults. He is expected to adjust to two totally different sets of rules and expectations. The need to be accepted by both parents can give way to feelings of inadequacy because he doesn't know what to do.

A new step-mom might think, "It is only natural that the child love his mother and would want to spend time with her. I want him to see her." Remember something: The more time you spend with your stepchild, knowing his need for love and assurance, the closer you become to him. And if your husband has full custody, you are the one he comes to when he is sick. You are the one who takes him to the doctor and gives him his medicine. He tells his needs to you. You buy his clothes and shoes. You see that he has his baths and that he eats right. You are the one who helps him with his homework and school parties. You give the encouragement and the discipline. You are the primary caregiver, and for all intents and purposes, you are a mother to this child. If you are in a situation where your stepchildren's mother does not see her children as often as she should, you in most cases automatically give your love to those children. It is not something you really think about doing. You just do it. You become protective of them and therefore do not like to see them hurt by anyone, not even their natural mother. People get used to seeing you in the role as "mom" to a child that is biologically someone else's. Strangers naturally assume that you are the child's mother, and those who know that you are the stepmother tend to "forget" that you are not the child's natural mother. As you struggle to keep the relationship on the basis of caretaker, friend, and step-mom, you constantly try to confirm your love for the child. If you have children of your own, you attempt to show no favoritism (always keep in mind the natural affection). When you don't feel especially loving to him, you tell him anyway, just as you would your own child. When a situation arises and the child is hurt, you try your best to help him. When he is upset by something his mother has done, or in many cases, has not done, you find yourself getting angry at her for hurting your (her) child. When she has confused the child about an issue of right and wrong, when she has disappointed him by canceling a visit, when she has tried to turn the child against his father or you by lies, you naturally want to shelter and protect him. The child, however, though hurt and confused, usually does not have the same feelings. He only knows that he loves his mother. He may not care what she has done and may actually condone her sin by blaming others. It is not uncommon for a child to feel that he is to blame. He may very well be angry at her for hurting or disappointing him, but remember, he may blame you just because you are there and his mother is not. And he may feel guilty for being angry at her. Your stepchild may rebuff your offers of love only to sparkle from the sporadic displays of affection she gives. A child cannot normally distinguish between the emotions as an adult can. But because of the selfish whims of a parent, the child now deals with feelings that strike to his very core.

These confusing sentiments carried by the child can perpetuate resentful feelings on the part of the stepmother.

This resentment can fester unless you make continual efforts to abort them. Is it easy to do? Is it always easy to remember not to take the negative feelings personally? Is it easy to unconditionally love another's child? Definitely not! But just being aware makes it somewhat less painful. Try to be empathetic. Put yourself in the child's place. How would you react to the separation and divorce of your parents? How would you react to seeing a stranger living in the same house with you, giving new rules, and setting new traditions? How would it be to automatically have new "brothers and sisters" that you don't know and don't want to know? What would it be like to be moved from one house into another with little or no warning? Everything in your life has changed and the most important person in your life is no longer there to greet you in the morning or kiss you goodnight before you go to bed.

Be willing to learn to forgive. Forgive his childishness, anger, confusion, and self-protectiveness. Be merciful to the child. Praying to God is the first of many ways to keep ill will from creeping into your home. Ask God to help you to keep a pure motive while dealing with your family. Pray for wisdom in handling each individual child. Ask the Lord to bless your home with peace. Above all, realize that divorce affects the child so deeply that even the child doesn't completely grasp the lingering consequences of what has taken place in his life.

Don't forget about communication. We don't always communicate with our children as we should. This takes time and effort. We cannot expect the child to do it. Sometimes it just takes sitting down and saying, "I feel like we have a problem. I'd like to talk about it with you." Just laying things out on the table will clear the air and can make the relationship more secure. The child needs to understand that you want to hear what he has to say. But remember: you must be big enough to accept what you hear. And don't expect it all to be good. You may hear some things that shock you and devastate you. But you also may hear the very thing you have been waiting to hear.

The role of stepmother is difficult. Sometimes you truly feel like giving up, wondering whatever made you think you could be successful in raising another's child. It is not so different from raising a child of your own, except that the natural affection is ever present with your own flesh and blood and the feelings for your stepchild are chosen feelings. This, in a sense, makes these feelings more special. When you choose to love someone you have to give more and try harder. It is normal to want to give unconditional love, compassion, friendship, or to show sincere interest in your biological child, but it is not quite as easy for you to have the same compassion or interest or to unconditionally love someone who has come into your life already a child or a teenager.

The Two May Be Spiritually Incompatible

From the beginning of time parents have planned, worried, and fretted over the choices of their children's mates. Abraham sent his personal servant in search of a wife for his son Isaac (Gen. 24). Isaac warned Jacob not to take a wife from the daughters of Canaan. Esau, on the other hand, chose ungodly women for his wives. As a result, his mother Rebekah was forever weary from the contention caused by these two women (Gen. 26:34-35; 27:46; 28:6-8).

We should be just as concerned for our children's future marriages. We should begin early teaching our children the importance of choosing the right mate. As parents we need to urge our children to date and marry those who are members of the church. But we must admit that no matter how much teaching or urging we do, a child may grow up and fall in love with a person that is not a member of the Lord's church. The young person may convince herself that it is nothing to be concerned about because they love each other. The young woman may convince herself that she can convert him. But once married the husband decides that going to church every Sunday morning, Sunday night, and Wednesday night is not appealing. He remembers that he went faithfully with her while they were dating, but things are different now. A friend calls and wants to go hunting. He surprises his new bride by trading his dress clothes for camouflage. She tries to convince him that worship is more important, but he insists that he deserves a break. This is just one example of the way situations that seemed to be perfect can change. The young bride has two alternatives: become unfaithful or remain faithful and go to church alone.

Remaining faithful to God is the primary goal for a Christian woman, especially if she is married to the non-Christian. It is not easy but it can be done. As a child I knew of a family of eight. The husband and wife were both non-Christians. She wanted to go to worship services and take the six children with her and her husband did not want her to go. He began early Sunday morning telling her that she could not go to church. She would calmly say, "I am going to church." He would argue and threaten and yell, telling her that if she went to church she would be sorry. She went to church. This continued each Sunday morning, Sunday night, and Wednesday evening for weeks. He then told her it was okay for her to go, but she could not take the children. Meekly and with a sweet nature, she went to church and took the children with her. One Sunday he changed his strategy. He told her that if she went to church, he would not be there when she returned. She was shocked at his threat but she did not waver. Alarmed at this new method of control, she looked at him and sadly said, "I love you and I will miss you if you decide to leave, but the children and I are going to church. I will be home at 12:30. I hope you change your mind." She arrived home as she told him she would and he was waiting for lunch. She was eventually baptized and soon all of her children followed her example. Though the husband has never obeyed the gospel he now offers to take her to church and returns to pick her up.

I realized when I was old enough to understand that being faithful is entirely an individual matter. There is no person on earth that can force one to become unfaithful. If she is dedicated from the day of her rebirth she will allow no one to deter her from living the Christian life. Only she has the ability to change her path.

The wife of a non-Christian has an abundance of problems to face. She may be married to a man who is a social or heavy drinker, a drug user, or an abuser. He may be a dedicated member of a denomination and insist their children be raised with his belief. Whatever the problems, the wife has many opportunities awaiting her. She has an opening like no other to teach her husband the gospel. When two people are as close as marriage brings them, the influence one has on the other is immeasurable. The non-Christian man knows the virtues of his Christian wife and most likely those are the very qualities that led him to marry her in the first place. He may have been taken by her meekness, firm beliefs, morals, her unswerving devotion, and her commitment. The Christian woman can influence her husband by being constant in her attendance to the services. She can influence him by being consistent with her stands for the truth. She can teach him by letting him see her pray, read her Bible, and helping those who need her. By being firmly grounded the wife can influence her husband by her conduct (1 Pet. 3:1). A Christian woman will try in whatever way she can to lead souls to Christ and that includes her husband. Many women have led their husbands to Christ merely by continuing to be steadfast in their lives as faithful children of God. A woman should not allow manipulation, intimidation, threats, ridicule, or cruel jokes to pressure her into leaving the church. The wife whose husband wants her to be unchristian-like so that he feels good about what he does is not obligated to grant that type of request. If a husband demands that you go to the bar with him because he wants to spend time with you, you do not have to go. Being submissive and obedient to God takes precedence over being submissive and obedient to the sinful dictates of an unbelieving husband. Numerous husbands have been led to Christ by the living example of their wives, and many will admit that had their wives given in just once, they would not have obeyed the gospel.

Faithfulness and commitment to one's spouse, regardless of his religious belief, is essential. One should never consider divorce because her spouse will not obey the gospel. Scripturally the only legitimate reason for divorce and remarriage is fornication. However, in some cases divorce does take place because the husband is of another faith or is just unhappy with a Christian wife. In 1 Corinthians 7:10-15 Paul deals with an unbelieving spouse departing from the believer. In verses 10 and 11 he says, "A wife is not to depart from her husband . . . And a husband is not to divorce his wife." The Greek word for *depart* is *choridzo*. The context of these two verses shows that *depart* and *divorce* mean the same thing. Therefore when a believer and unbeliever are bound to each other through the vows of marriage, they should not seek a divorce. They should work at making their marriage as happy and fulfilling as they can. If, however, the unbeliever will not stay with you because of your Christianity and your refusal to live like he does, then the Bible teaches to let him leave (v. 15). Sad as this situation is, remarriage for the child of God is not an option if the unbeliever is not guilty of fornication. Very few people want to accept this passage as it is stated. They want to add these verses when trying to prove there is more than one reason for divorce and remarriage. They do so by taking verse 15 and saying, "Here it is. It says that 'if the unbeliever departs,' I am 'not under bondage in such cases.'" *Not under bondage* only means that the brother or sister is not bound to obey the ungodly whims, requests, or demands made on them by the unbelieving spouse. Thus is the case with a husband who demands that his wife participate in drinking, drug use, or immorality. For the Christian in this situation, sympathy is deeply felt. But if there is no immorality involved the two are still husband and wife in the eyes of God.

PART THREE

Children

6

The Danger of Worldliness:
Safeguards for Our Children
Cindy Colley

Love not the world, neither the things that are in the world. If any man love the world, the love of the Father is not in him. For all that is in the world, the lust of the flesh, and the lust of the eyes, and the pride of life, is not of the Father, but is of the world (1 John 2:15-16).

I am convinced that the greatest enemy of the church, as we look to a new century, attacks from within. As I travel to speak in various parts of the country, I never cease to be amazed at the thoroughness of the world's saturation into the Lord's church. I do believe that it is vitally important that parents in the church today take extreme measures to guard the hearts and lives of our children against the dangers of worldliness. But, frankly, I see little hope of instilling in the minds of our children what is largely lacking in the hearts of their parents. If I, as a parent, do not recognize the world as my enemy and draw practical lifestyle lines that distinguish me from the world, it is highly unlikely that my children will. We are already at least a generation behind in defeating our greatest enemy. As we think about worldliness, let us begin with a heart of self-examination, remembering that the criterion for this soul search is not the prevailing standards of the society around us, but the Word of God.

What is meant by the world in 1 John 2:15-16? The Greek word used is *kosmos,* meaning a system or an order. Sometimes I think the reason we have such a problem with worldliness in the church is that we fail to recognize it as an enemy. We tend to think about the world as the beautiful earth that is our home. Perhaps we think of the world as the six billion people that inhabit it. But neither of these is the *kosmos* of 1 John 2:15-16. This *kosmos* is a system in the same sense that we might speak of "the world of sports," or "the world of finance."

The world is a system in that it is directed by the calculating leadership of a prince. John 12:31 calls Satan, the ruler of this ungodly system, the prince of this world. (Other passages that describe Satan this way are John 14:30 and John 16:11.) The administrator of this order is not to be trusted. He is the father of lies (John 8:44). He is not a sleeping giant to be ignored. He is vigilantly walking about as a lion, seeking whom he may devour (1 Pet. 5:8).

The world is a system with a distinct philosophy. It is based on an enticing network of values and ideas skillfully woven together to make an attractive presentation. First Corinthians 2:12 speaks of the "spirit of this world." First Corinthians 3:19 talks of the "wisdom of this world," while 1 Corinthians 7:31 speaks of the "fashion of this world." The world is not merely the happenings of the populace around us. The world consists of the calculated efforts of a prince and his followers to promote a well-defined philosophy.

The philosophy of the world can best be defined when we look at the purpose of the world. The world's goal is to oppose Christ and to disgrace His followers. This purpose is stated in the following verses:

> The world cannot hate you; but me it hateth, because I testify of it, that the works thereof are evil (John 7:7).

> Even the Spirit of truth; whom the world cannot receive, because it seeth him not, neither knoweth him: but ye know

him; for he dwelleth with you, and shall be in you (John 14:17).

If the world hate you, ye know that it hated me before it hated you (John 15:18).

As we realize that the purpose of the world is opposition to Christ, we understand that any prevailing idea that undermines the Word of God or the work of His kingdom is of the world.

The sobering personal question then is: Who are the people of this world? I know that as a Christian, I cannot be of this world. James 4:4 tells me that if I am a friend of this world I am the enemy of God. In reality, if I am friendly with the values of this system, if I fail to oppose with my life, my words, and my influence, the ideology of the prince of this world, I am the friend of the world and the enemy of God.

So how do I identify worldliness around me?

A Clear Statement from the World

In the year 1933, a group of men drafted a document entitled *Humanist Manifesto*. While you may not be familiar with this text, it is an important part of our discussion because it articulates the spirit of worldliness in our age. Many people believe that this document, which rejects the existence of a creator and establishes man as the center of existence, has wreaked havoc in our society. With this manifesto, Satan actually was just putting a new face on the age-old mentality that rejects God and elevates man to his position. (Remember, Satan is the prince. His administrative job is to keep policies in place to oppose Christ and His followers.) Consider a brief quotation from *Humanist Manifesto I*:

> Religious Humanism considers the complete realization of human personality to be the end of man's life and seeks its development in the here and now. This is the explanation

of the humanist's social passion . . . In place of the old attitudes involved in worship and prayer, the humanist finds his religious emotions expressed in a heightened sense of personal life and in a cooperative effort to promote social well being.

Humanism is self-described as a religion. Obvious in its foundational principles is the direct and vehement opposition to Christ. Thus, it is worldliness. It is not difficult to figure out that when we reject God and elevate man to the center of existence, we ascribe to Satan's system and thus, we are of this world.

Sometimes more difficult to recognize as worldliness are the more subtle influences, the gradual changes that occur around us that are products of humanism. How has it affected the sphere of influences that mold our children? What are practical precautions that we, as mothers, can take to guard their hearts from the philosophies that spring from humanism? It is the purpose of this lesson to put up some red flags for mothers who are conscientiously attempting to keep their children unspotted from the world (James 1:27).

Voices from the World

Prevalent beliefs about human origins are attempting to undermine the faith that we work so hard to instill within our children. I was recently having a conversation with a very close friend about her daughter, who is in her mid teens, and has not obeyed the gospel. They make sure that she is present for every service. The family's involvement in the work of the church is consistent. They are benevolent and evangelistic. I was shocked to hear my friend say that the underlying reason for her daughter's unresponsiveness to the gospel was that she doubts the existence of God. This is not the first time that I have had sincere and devout Christian parents who, somewhere in the teen years, face the cold reality that their faith has not been transferred.

We teach our children that they are to listen intently to the subject matter at school, that they are to respect their teachers, and we expect good report cards to reflect that they are absorbing the material presented. They are conditioned to equate textbook information with truth. The theory of organic evolution is presented in American schools as the literal beginning point of textbook truth! This theory of origins affects the presentation of materials in all areas of study. It should come as no shock to us that our children have difficulty maintaining faith in the Creator, when the scholarly world of academia shouts to them that He is a myth. How can they keep from being confused when they begin the day in homeroom quoting the phrase, "one nation under God," and then proceed to history and science classes in which His very existence is denied?

Mothers, this is where you must become a piece of the puzzle in the development of your child's faith! We must show our children these evidences! The time has passed when we can assume that two hours a week in Bible classes, that sometimes never even address evidences of creation, can successfully combat thirty hours a week in classes that are textually based on the opposing theory. Our challenge is enormous and we must diligently and persistently present to our children a scholarly refutation of the prevailing theories of origins.

This begins at an early age by presenting the creation story until they know it in detail. It includes constant discussion as you encounter the wonders of God's creation. Talk with them about the marvels of plant life, animal life, and human life. Notice the intricate workings of the details of the human body. While they are young, continually speak of the amazing design of our universe and of the necessity of an intelligent designer. This design/designer principle is one that they will see at work in all observable areas of life. It is a universal, scientific principle that will erect an early blockade against the theory of evolution. It will be very valuable later on.

As they become older, make sure they have access to printed research that points to the existence of God. Some of the best of these materials are available from Apologetics Press at 230 Landmark Drive in Montgomery, Alabama. Your tax dollars are already paying for the presentation of evolution to your children. Surely Christian parents want to invest in materials written by scientists who provide compelling arguments for the existence of God.

If your children attend public school, you cannot afford to be uninformed or uninvolved in their curricula. We can no longer feel secure in relegating the education of our children to others. The training and education of our children has always been a parental responsibility (Deut. 6:7; Eph. 6:4). Even if I share this process with others, I am ultimately responsible for its means and end. The buck stops with parents. I must know what my children are studying. I must study along with them, so that they will be able to recognize and refute false teachings, and I must support them and stand with them as they stand for the Scriptures in a challenging arena.

At this point, I would also point out that public education is not the only option. Many Christian parents have chosen to establish or participate in private educational institutions, based on the Word of God and His values system. More and more are choosing home schooling, an option that is both legal and statistically credible from an academic standpoint. More important, parents who are willing to make this large time commitment are directly involved in the education process. Those who choose this kind of direct involvement should be supported by elderships and fellow Christians. For those who may be interested in home schooling, there is a large network of home schoolers within the church already in place. (Contact: Mark McWhorter, 420 Chula Vista Mountain Road, Pell City, Alabama 35125; 205-338-1843.)

Remember, parental involvement is the key to faith maintenance. A child left to himself bringeth his mother shame (Prov. 29:15).

Materialism follows quickly on the heels of a rejection of God. As the *Manifesto* clearly states, without the existence of God and the hope of an afterlife, fulfillment can only occur in the here and now. Things temporal are the only things. How quickly our children adapt to the materialistic society in which we live!

Materialism is worldliness. Although materialism is discussed elsewhere in this book, I want to address it for a moment specifically in reference to our children. I am quite amazed as I interact with my children and their friends at the prevailing attitude of ingratitude. When my children have guests they sometimes complain about the food I have prepared or the restaurant that we have chosen. While they feel quite free to express their preferences, they do not so freely express their gratitude. I am sure that these symptoms of ingratitude occur in our children today because our society has placed self at the center. We have been so richly blessed in America that we take our affluence for granted and sometimes even murmur as He blesses us.

I believe that materialism is a part of Satan's system. He is aware that our children cannot serve God and mammon (Matt. 6:24). He knows that if he can make our children fall in love with things, that he can draw them from God. What are some practical ways in which I can combat his effort on this front?

I can teach my children the joy of giving at a very young age. It is more blessed to give than to receive (Acts 20:35). If I involve my children constantly in making little gifts or gathering flowers or baking bread for other people, they will grow up with a giving heart. Opportunities to give abound. Hostess gifts, benevolence programs through the local congregation, birthdays of the elderly, missionaries, and goody bags for Christian college students are just a few ideas for lessons in giving. This is a blessedness that I can add to their lives, just by letting them have a hand in the simple pleasure of giving.

I can teach my children to say thank you. First, I must teach them the ritual of the magic words, *please* and *thank you,* each time an object is handed to them. Later, I diligently insist that they write thank-you notes to those who give them gifts or entertain them. When we travel and enjoy hospitality in homes, the rule is to say thank you to the lady of the house following the meal and to each member of the household as we leave the home. Then a note of gratitude follows when we are back home again. The mealtime thank-you rule applies at home, as well.

I can refrain from murmuring about the blessings of God. If I complain about the rain, God's life sustaining blessing of water, how should I expect my children to refrain from complaining about the mere human kindnesses that are extended to them from others?

I can teach them the responsibilities of stewardship. From a very young age, we must teach our children to purpose weekly and give to God accordingly. They need to think of any monies they have accumulated that week, whether it was a gift, an allowance, or earned money. Then they need to decide an appropriate amount to give to God and set that aside before spending or depositing to savings accounts. At our house, this amount is never less than ten percent. The point of purposing is to make them realize the goodness of God and that He is the source of all material blessings.

As children mature, I can teach the responsibilities of stewardship by requiring responsibility regarding purchases. My son has a neighborhood trash-can business. He takes cans to the street on garbage pickup day and returns them to garages after the truck runs. His earnings are modest, but he is required to buy his own tennis shoes from the profits. The first pair he bought was the latest style from the biggest name brand manufacturer. They had the biggest price tag. He ouched a little as he spent the big bucks on those tennis shoes. Those shoes represented a lot of retrieved trash cans. He outgrew them quickly and on the second go-around, decided that a sale pair of quality shoes from a local salvage shoe store was a smarter purchase. He was learning, at least on some level, that it's smart to look further than the item that I am purchasing—the fulfillment of the desires of here and now—that it's important to also consider the amount I am saving for something more important, perhaps more meaningful than the right logo. All of this learning must be done within the framework of always seeking the kingdom first.

I can and must teach my children the practical principles of James 2:1-5. My children must never be allowed to shun or make fun of anyone who doesn't have the right clothes. My daughter came home from an outing with church friends recently and reported to me that someone commented about an outfit she was going to wear (which was perfectly modest and neat). "Are you sure you want to wear that?" they said. At this time we talked together about what James said in these verses. We talked about our God who looks upon the heart. I am convinced that we, as parents, need to have such conversations more often.

The primary and most important thing that I can do to guard my children from materialism is to shift the material things of this life to their proper place in my own life. I have a tremendous opportunity to do this when I, as a mother, choose to make material sacrifices in order to be a keeper at home (Titus 2:5). No rhetoric about materialism will be as effective as this distinctive lifestyle. No gift that money could buy will be of such great value to them.

Rampant sexual impurity has also been an attendant in the procession of humanism through our society. I recently was informed about a blood drive that occurred at a high school near my home. The school was not located in a metropolitan area, but rather in small town Alabama. Out of those students who volunteered to give blood, fifty percent were turned away because they tested positive for the HIV virus. As I talk with Christian girls in our community, they reveal to me that virginity among their peers is not nearly as common as promiscuity; that the girls who are considered good at school are those who are sexually active with only one partner. While my first reaction to their revelations is shock, my second is to question my shock. We are talking about children who have been taught that they evolved from lower life forms. They have grown up in a society that largely denies that there is an authoritative power from which we originated. Values taught separately from the Word of God result in the final message that each individual is responsible for the determination of right and wrong for himself. If they are convinced that they are merely advanced forms of animal life, void of soul or future destiny, why shouldn't they behave as the animals do? Why am I shocked that our society moves ever further from sexual restraint?

Again we see that the system of Satan works. The sad truth is, that the loss of sexual inhibitions that has occurred in the world has affected and continues to affect young people within the church. Even young people with good intentions and conscientious hearts find themselves in situations where they are tempted to compromise their convictions about purity. As one young girl recently told me in describing the difficulties of high school dating, "Even the good boys expect and feel comfortable with things that hurt my conscience as a Christian."

For too long, Christian parents have been embarrassed to discuss the specifics of dating with their children. We tell them to be pure, but we fail to give them the tools that they need to maintain their purity. I understand that sensitive matters about sexuality are difficult to address with our children. I confess that I am embarrassed to talk about them. But I am not so embarrassed that I will fail to talk to my daughter about the specific safeguards that she can take to avoid situations of compromise. I wish that the world was still embarrassed by these matters. But the world has lost the ability to blush (Jer. 6:15). And while we have found it uncomfortable to talk about sexual purity with our children, the media and their peers have been quite open with the opposite message. It is time that we talk frankly with our children about the particulars of purity.

Decisions about sin are always easier made before temptation presents itself. Parents should encourage young people to make early decisions about where they will and will not go. They should decide well before the dating years that they will not go to parties where alcoholic beverages are being served. One reason is that sexual inhibitions are loosened by alcohol consumption. Our children should decide that they will not attend dances before they are even invited to do so. They should be taught that the meaning of lasciviousness in Galatians 5:19-21 includes indecent bodily movements and unchaste handling of males and females. They should decide that they will not go swimming or sunning in today's beachwear in mixed company because of passages like 1 Timothy 2:9 and Matthew 5:28. They should have standards well in advance of dating that will prohibit them from going to see movies that have provocative sexual scenes, nudity, or the portrayal of flippant or illicit sex. I must help my children decide that they will not be left alone, that is, in a locked house, in a parked secluded car, or in a closed bedroom with their dates. It will be far easier to prevent unwanted advances if definite boundaries have been firmly set in their minds. One teenager recently confided in me that she wished her boyfriend's parents had not left them alone in their home so often. Wise parents are committed to maintaining the fences around the hearts of their children.

On a very personal level, parents should discuss with their children some definite boundaries about touching. They should decide ahead of time that they will never remove articles of clothing in the presence of members of the opposite sex. They should be given specific guidelines about hugging and kissing that will help them to avoid sexual arousal. I intend to talk to my children in specific terms about what is appropriate touching and what is lasciviousness. I am going to emphasize to my daughter that any forwardness on her part may be interpreted as an invitation for sexual misconduct. I want her to be unwilling to initiate advances, and always to be fully in control of the boundaries. I want both of my children to know before they ever leave on a date, that when faced with the temptation to commit fornication, the best defense is a good pair of running shoes and the King's highway! If they even begin to feel that they are in a compromising situation, they shouldn't take the time to talk it over or wait around to see if it feels right; they should vacate the premises. The Bible says it concisely: Flee fornication (1 Cor. 6:18). I want them to have the image of Joseph in Genesis 39 clearly imprinted on their hearts. He left his coat and fled. I want my daughter to always have a telephone number where someone can be reached should she decide she needs a way home.

All of these seem to me to be common sense suggestions. The discussions we have with our children should always be prefaced with the truth that God's sexual restrictions are not intended to keep sex from them, but rather to keep sex for them. They should anticipate fulfilling sexual relationships within the marriage relationship.

Which Voice Will They Hear?

Since Satan is the father of lies, he baits his hooks for our children with colorful and attractive myths. That's why the evolution myth is presented to them in an acceptable classroom format. That's why our world equates success and money. That's why we hear so much about safe sex. He offers an instant heaven and delivers an eternal hell.

Parents are key players in the mind games that Satan plays with our children. We are the ones who can peel back the glitter of the world and show them the face value of every card the devil holds. But I can't expose him to my children if he is still holding the cards and I am still playing his game. They will be unable to hear me for the noise of the game around me. I cannot remain fashioned according to this world (Rom. 12:2), while successfully calling my children to a life of sacrifice (v. 1). "Wherefore, come out from among them and be ye separate, saith the Lord" (2 Cor. 6:17).

7

What Mothers Can Do
Cindy Colley

"The rod and reproof give wisdom but a child left to himself bringeth his mother to shame" (Prov. 29:15)

One thousand unwed teenage girls become pregnant each day in America. Four thousand, two hundred and nineteen teens contract sexually transmitted diseases daily. Today five hundred adolescents will become drug users while one thousand will take their first drink of beverage alcohol. One hundred and thirty-five thousand children carry weapons to school daily, so it comes as no surprise that thirty-six hundred teens will be assaulted. This number includes eighty who will be raped. Twenty-two hundred children will drop out of school and six precious lives will be lost to suicide. (Statistics are from the Children's Defense Fund and the book, *13th Generation,* by Neil Howe and Bill Strauss.)

Statistics are startling, but the events of our local papers are even more disturbing. In the metropolitan area near my home, fornication recently occurred in a middle school classroom between two thirteen-year-olds while the teacher was present in the classroom. Fences have been erected in football stadiums in this city to separate fans of opposing teams. Officials hope to avoid the violence and even killing that was occurring between fans over the outcome of what was designed to be a recreational activity. School uniforms are worn in many school systems of our

country, but in our area they are worn to stop the occurrences of children killing children over something so trivial
as a pair of Nikes. At the homecoming halftime festivities
at our local middle school last year, students watched as
the queen they had chosen by popular vote was crowned.
She was six months pregnant.

How have we reached this point in which daytime cur-
fews for children are becoming the norm in many cities
and teen pregnancy is often a status symbol? More importantly, what are the answers to the cataclysmic circumstances that face our children as we round the bend of the
millennium?

I cannot single-handedly solve all of the problems that
face the youth of our nation. The fall of this Humpty
Dumpty has been great and he is extremely shattered.
There is One, though, who does know all of the answers
for all of the ills that have ever faced mankind in any dis-
pensation. He knows the answers for young people in
America today. He knows the answers for parents in
America today. Although I believe that the challenges of
godly motherhood are greater today than they have been
in American history, God knows the answers for me, personally, as I attempt to raise children who will rise above
the society in which they live.

God has given us, in his Word, some very basic truths
about parenting that have been largely ignored by a generation of parents. When any society ignores the plan of
God, grievous consequences are incurred. Likewise, it is
only in the recognition of His will and the return to His
Word in our daily lives that the downward spiral can stop.
This happens one home at a time. America, in a real sense,
determines its destiny one mother at a time. I cannot cure
all of the ills that plague the youth of America today. But
let me do what I *can* do. Let me never fail to do what I
must do within my home, my greatest sphere of influence.
Keenly feeling the responsibility inherent in motherhood,
I offer these suggestions for godly motherhood. They are

based on a love for the will of God, for the two precious souls with which He has entrusted me, and for the thoughtful readers of this chapter.

1. Pray in Your Home

Like Manoah, the father of Samson, I should pray before my children are even born, *Lord, teach us what we shall do unto the child that shall be born* (Judg. 13:8). Certainly, as a Christian mother, I want to invoke His richest blessings upon every day of their lives. What do I pray for in regard to my children?

I pray for wisdom as a mother. In James 1:5, we are given an amazing prayer promise. It says that if I lack wisdom, I should ask God to supply my deficit. It goes on to say that because He is a God who gives to all people liberally and does not upbraid, He will give me a liberal portion of heavenly wisdom! Which of us as mothers today can afford to pass up this amazing offer?

I pray for each child by name. I pray for specific needs, distinctive phases of life, and particular challenges of each of my children. When they are young I am sure that they actually hear me speak their names before the Father's throne. I make sure that they hear their father and me pray that they will grow up to be Christians. I believe that when they go away to college, they will remember the prayer vigil of Christian parents and that they will find strength in that memory.

I pray for another girl and boy. My daughter, Hannah, knows that I pray daily for that little boy, wherever he may be, who will one day grow up to be her husband. I pray for the parents who are raising him and for the direction of his life. My son, Caleb, has heard many prayers offered for the girl who will one day be his wife. Because I believe the marriage decision is extremely critical to the happiness and ultimate salvation of my children and because I know that God superintends in the affairs of his faithful children, I find great comfort in this prayer. I believe that my children are being impressed with the gravity of the commitment of marriage as they know I'm praying for their future homes.

2. Take Advantage of Everyday Opportunities to Teach Your Children about God.

In the sixth chapter of Deuteronomy, God told His people of old that there was a way they could insure that their sons and their son's sons would fear the Lord, keeping His statutes and His commandments (v. 2). That kind of insurance is very interesting to me in a generation where Christian parents lose over half of their children to the world. I read on. In verse 5, I find that the first injunction for those parents was to love the Lord *themselves* with all of their hearts, souls, and might. Verse 7 is the key passage for our observation:

> And thou shalt teach them diligently unto thy children, and shalt talk of them when thou sittest in thine house, and when thou walkest by the way, and when thou liest down, and when thou risest up.

The only time I should talk of God's precepts with my children if I really want them to walk in His statutes is when we are sitting, when we are moving, when we are going to bed, and when we are getting up! That's all!

Obviously, the first prerequisite in the installation of faith within the tender hearts of my children is time with them. Given the working conditions of most families in America today, the kind of time required by this passage is an impossibility. But God said that it is time spent together with His statutes as the central theme of daily living that will produce faithful children. Mothers of today desperately need to examine priorities, question motives, and search souls before delegating large portions of their daily parenting hours to other people. When I fail to protect my time and allow materialism to dictate my schedule, I'm sacrificing a very precious insurance benefit. The insurance plan of Deuteronomy 6 requires large and frequent installments of time.

The commitment of time must be followed by the wisest expenditures of that time. I am convinced that God gives mothers a wealth of teaching resources every day if we will only open our eyes to them. When you have baked rolls or loaves of bread, have you ever discussed with your children the story of Elijah and the widow of Zarephath who was blessed with perpetual ingredients for baking when she ministered to God's prophet (1 Kings 17)? Have you talked with them about Jesus, the bread of life? When you see the pretty flowers in the yard or by the roadside, do you take the time to tell them how God clothes the lilies of the field and that He cares so much more for them (Matt. 6:28-30)? Wouldn't it be a shame to let a rainbow go by without telling them of a faithful God who keeps His promises (Gen. 7), or to experience a storm without talking about the One who made even the winds and the sea to obey Him? When you are scrubbing the stains from laundry or from the kitchen counter, do you tell them of the stains of sin and the one cleansing agent for removing those stains (1 John 1:7)? The possibilities are endless and the opportunities are eternal! The key is to remember that it is an all day, everyday process—one that nurtures a practical relationship with the Father for a lifetime.

A daily *family time* centered around God's Word is also an invaluable faith-building tool.

This time should include everyone in the family and should be a predictable priority. The lifestyle of our busy family demands that we sometimes have this devotional time in the van on the way home from some activity. We usually begin by singing songs that are understandable and appropriate for the age levels of our children. Many times the songs we sing are Scriptures set to music. Then we discuss a certain account from the Bible in words that our children can understand, or perhaps we read a letter from a missionary with whom we correspond. We often let the children play competitive games that test their Bible knowledge. Sometimes we even have prizes! The discussion often turns to a particular question or challenge they faced on that day as they tried to live for Jesus before their friends. But always the time we share ends with thanksgiving and petitions to God. Finding the time to set aside for this is difficult, but those who have done it know that it is far more than a ritual. It is a relevant and very practical way to be sure that God lives at my house.

3. Make Sure You Bring Your Children to Every Bible Class and Worship Service.

Sometimes I think as parents we fail to realize the lifetime impact that the seemingly small decisions we make about priorities have upon our children. Matthew 6:33, when paired with Hebrews 10:25, must set a practical standard in my home for faithful attendance to worship if I expect my children to be faithful adults. These verses say:

> But seek ye first the kingdom of God, and his righteousness; and all these things shall be added unto you.

> Not forsaking the assembling of ourselves together, as the manner of some is; but exhorting one another: and so much the more, as ye see the day approaching.

I recently read about a disease called congenital analgesia. Found mostly in children, the disease causes the inability to feel pain in nerve endings. At first glance the inability to feel pain might seem a good thing. But pain is the warning signal that directs our bodies away from danger. Children who have this disease are constantly burning their hands and feet, and breaking bones because they are unaware of impending danger. It occurred to me as I heard of this malady that as a parent I can cause my children to develop *spiritual* analgesia, a condition in which my children can become spiritually unhealthy, and perhaps even die, without ever feeling the pain of impending danger.

Think with me about parents who consider themselves to be faithful members of the church. Perhaps they are active in its programs and can generally be depended upon to show up for the worship assembly. They do not miss worship for sports, unless it is a really big game—perhaps a tournament game. They do not allow their children to put schoolwork in front of Wednesday evening Bible classes—unless it is a really big exam on Thursday. They come even when they are tired. It would really be a rare thing for them to miss a service just because they had a hard day at work. They really are there almost every time. Their percentages really are quite good.

And then the kids go off to college. How many nights of the week at the university do you suppose there's a really big sports activity going on? How often is there a big exam the next morning? How often at seven at night do you think they are *really* tired? The answers are obvious. Tough choices are daily occurrences. But these kids have been conditioned to be able to miss worship services under certain conditions without feeling the pain. The *conditions* just become more and more frequent and so eventually the children rarely or never attend worship at all, and the spiritual divorce was practically painless!

I want to condition my children to feel pain should they ever forsake the worship hour. I want them to be unable to remember a single time when the saints were meeting in our congregation when we chose to be elsewhere. It may mean missing practices, rehearsals, games, and even school functions, but their presence at these activities will not matter one iota in a few short years. Keeping their hearts tender to Matthew 6:33, the *priority passage,* will make an eternal difference. An obvious side benefit of prioritizing in this way is the wonderful opportunity children have to develop courage and evangelism skills as they explain to coaches, directors, teammates, and teachers that Christ and His church are *the* prior commitment, above all others.

4. Develop Spiritual Family Projects.

All too often we, as mothers, especially if our husbands are preachers or elders, have a tendency to speak of "Daddy's work in the church" or "Daddy's preaching job." While it may be true that Daddy is the one who is employed by the local church, the businesses of evangelism, benevolence, and edification are the shared responsibility of all of the members of the church and thus, all of the members of my family. It should come as no shock to those of us who refer to *church work* as an adult activity when our children somehow never assume the Lord's work as a personal responsibility.

There are endless opportunities to involve our children in His cause. Let me share just a few ideas:

- Choose a missionary with whom you can correspond. Have your children write personal letters or send e-mail messages to him. Encourage them to occasionally send small gifts from their piggy banks. A missionary with children is especially interesting to the young ones. Help them think of cultural as well as spiritual questions to ask. You will be amazed at how excited your children will become to learn of baptisms that have occurred in some remote area of the world. They will feel a part of foreign evangelism.

- Make a widow assignment. Tell your children that before sitting down each time they attend worship services, they must each find three widows to hug and greet. If you attend a larger congregation, make a stipulation that they can't choose the same three ladies twice in a row. There is a wealth of untouched wisdom and influence when our children get to know faithful elderly saints.

- Challenge each family member to learn one hundred verses of Scripture each year. Say them to each other in blocks of ten verses or, for a challenge, in two sessions saying fifty verses each.

- Have your children choose someone from the congregation's sick list to whom he can send a card each week. Cards to those who become Christians or place membership can also be a part of this project.

- Have non-Christians over for meals. Make sure your children know that the reason you want to get to know these people is because you hope to share Jesus with them. Let your children help clean the house and fix the food. Make sure you pray together for the occasion. Pray that hearts will be open to learning His will.

Of course this list is endless. Child involvement in the spiritual aspects of family living is the emphasis here. Spiritually involved children grow into spiritual adults!

5. Monitor the Media.

The television in your living room can be enemy number one as you attempt to raise godly children. I am literally amazed as I travel about and speak for ladies' groups at the entertainment that many Christians find acceptable on television and at the movies. I am sure that we would not allow anyone to stand in our homes and use the foul language that we invite into our living rooms via the television set.* We would be shocked and disgusted were folks to behave sexually before us as we allow them to behave on the screen before our eyes. We've come to somehow believe that it is less damaging if we watch it on a screen.

Another myth we have come to believe is that if Hollywood produces it, we must see it. I have actually heard Christians defend the watching of vulgar materials with this statement: "But nothing else was on." It is later than you think. Conscientious parents must realize that *on* is not the only television option. When material that flies in the face of morality and Christian values appears on television sets in Christian homes, there should be an unquestioned consistency in the response. The offending show should always be turned off.

I also watch with wonder the response of Christians, in general, to the movie industry. Movies that carry ratings of PG, PG-13, or R are so rated because they contain some incident or language or storyline that will be offensive to someone. If that *someone* is not a Christian, then who should it be? We need to be offended by the sexual content, the homosexuality, the nudity, the profanity, and the violence that make movies unsuitable for general audiences.

A popular film was the largest money-making movie in history. It seems that all the world saw it. It was rated PG-13 and did contain offensive material,

*Editor's Note: A device called *TV Guardian* automatically filters out (mutes) foul language from closed captioned TV shows and movies. This device is easy to install and reasonably priced. Far more important, however, is the fact that it removes offensive language from your TV. This device may be ordered from Sunrise Family Video, 135 North 100 East, American Fork, Utah 84003, 801-756-6726.

including nudity. As I am involved with Christian young people both at home and as I travel, I hear them converse frequently about the movie, many of them having seen it more than once. I wonder about how Christian parents have come to the point that even such nudity is acceptable viewing if all the world is doing it. I worry about future generations when these children will be the parents. I wonder if Paul's call to *be not conformed to this world* (Rom.12:2) will have any practical application at all by that time. I'm perplexed about how we apply the admonition of 1 Thessalonians 5:22 which says, "Abstain from every appearance of evil." I am sure that we are reaching the place when we condition our children to *rejoice in iniquity* (1 Cor. 13:6).

It is true that I cannot singlehandedly change the movie industry. But I can refrain from buying the corruption of my children. It is time for Christian mothers to hear the wake-up call. Satan must be laughing at our hypocrisy when we despair about the wicked world in which our children are growing up while we pay for their exposure to glamorized immorality.

6. Discipline Your Children Firmly and with Love.

A century ago it seems there was little confusion about the difference between loving discipline, including corporal punishment, and child abuse. Psychologists though, a generation ago, muddied this water by telling us that loving parents don't spank. They even warned us that spanking contributes to aggressive behavior and teaches the lesson that "I can win because I am bigger and stronger than you."

Today, out of the chaos of a generation of children who have grown up largely without restraint, we are once again hearing voices of the experts, many of whom have come full circle to the acknowledgment that there is such a thing as loving, productive spanking and that the generation that grew up without its benefits were deprived of some valuable lessons about respect for authority.

God is an advocate of corporal punishment. "The rod and reproof give wisdom" (Prov. 29:15). "He that spareth the rod hateth his son: but he that loveth him chasteneth him betimes" (Prov.13:24). What a blessing for mothers as we try to prepare our children for use in His service that we can look to the Manufacturer's directions and know that consistent, loving spanking is a necessary and right approach to the discipline challenges we face with our children. Often when I express this in lectures, there will be someone who takes issue with this position about spanking. I am so happy to be able to tell them that God is the original advocate of spanking.

God is the Creator of all children and He knows their needs. As a responsible Christian mother, I respect His will regarding the discipline of my children. I spank them because He told me to do it. But, on a practical level, I can surely see the positive results of this consistent, loving form of discipline. Sometimes withholding privileges because of bad behavior and offering rewards for good behavior may be appropriate measures. Parents must remember, though, that these incentives, while they may be effective, take more diligence to administer. I may have taken away privileges on Monday, and by Friday be weary of enforcing Monday's punishment. I must be careful to carry out the consequences that are now separated by time from the offense. Spanking, on the other hand, says it all at once: "Your behavior was wrong. Because you disobeyed me, I am going to punish you." Once the spanking is delivered, the incident is over and you can get on with the business of the day.

No forms of discipline work if they are not administered consistently. If I promise a spanking if a child violates a command, I must deliver it. If a particular action is wrong and punishable today, it must be wrong and punishable tomorrow. Inconsistency in discipline is worse than a failure to discipline, for it sends a message of confusion and unfairness.

Punishment, especially spanking, should never be administered in a fit of rage. I may often be upset by defiance or disobedience, but my response must always be calm and controlled.

Sometimes it may be necessary to wait a moment to collect my thoughts before responding to an action. Chastening is a disagreeable task, but one that yields the peaceable fruit of righteousness within the home (Heb. 12:11). If this fruit is my constant objective, my chastening will always be from a heart of love. As I read Hebrews 12, I am reminded that it is *not* a heart of love that would allow a child to continue down a path of defiance that ultimately leads to sorrow and sin.

Each time I allow my child to wilfully disobey without consequences, I am withholding a valuable lesson about respect for authority. I am losing an opportunity to lead him to respect the ultimate authority of God.

7. Teach Your Children to Respect Their Father.

Assuming that your spouse is worthy of respect, it is vital that you show respect for his leadership at all times. Passages regarding your submission in the home are abundant. In a world in which feminism would destroy the time-honored and biblical role of women in the home, it is imperative that you show a joyful spirit of submission and respect before your children. You can be assured that their faithfulness in regard to roles within the home will be challenged in our society. We, as mothers, must show them that God's way continues to be the best way.

Like so many aspects of Christian living, this is an all-day, everyday undertaking. When your husband comes home from work in the afternoon, don't grumble, "Oh no, Daddy's here and look at this mess and I bet he's going to be hungry, too." Say, "Look! Daddy's home and aren't we glad to see him!" Don't criticize him in front of the children. When there are disagreements between the two of you, try to choose private places to discuss them. Never let your children hear you raise your voice to him. Support him in any decision that is within the will of God.

Feminism shouts selfishness to our little girls. They *will* be bombarded by the world's message about assertiveness. One of Satan's most effective tools in the late twentieth century has been to alter God's plan for the woman in the home. He knows that if he can successfully rob homes of submissive wives and godly mothers that he can win generations to come. It is up to parents to combat the devil on this front by portraying the beauty of respect and the order that comes from filling the roles that He ordained within the home.

Conclusion

Time is of the essence. Even as I wrote this chapter, America was shaken by the deaths of five innocent people in a middle school shooting in Jonesboro, Arkansas. If there has ever been a time to panic about the moral plunge of our young people, the time is now. If there are things that you, as a mother, intend to do to give your children an anchor of faith in this uncertain society, now is the time to do them.

Time is of the essence. I am convinced of the value of each suggestion made in this chapter. I believe that each of them will make contributions to the spiritual foundations that you and I are trying to build. I believe they will have an eternal impact and that destinies can be influenced by their implementation. But the catch is, they all take time. Time is the common factor in the equation of bringing up righteous children. And time seems to be the one commodity that is in shortest supply in our society.

Eighteen short years is about all I can expect to really have my children with me. That's only a fourth of a normal lifespan. It's just a speck in eternity. And yet the decisions of those few short years play a major role in the molding and shaping of a precious soul for eternity. The reality of the brevity of my time with my children, coupled with the magnitude of my influence on them, demands that my decisions about time spent with them be carefully weighed. May I remember that the insurance policy is purchased with frequent and large installments of time.

PART FOUR

Current Issues

8

A Place of Honor:
The Role of Women in the
Work of the Church
Jane McWhorter

The winds of change were blowing ever so gently in 1973 when I included a chapter on "Woman's Limitations" in the book *She Hath Done What She Could*.[10] In the distance was the faint rumbling of thunder as various denominations began placing women in leadership positions due to the demands of the Feminist Movement. Although I alluded to such practices in that book, it was not a problem in the Lord's church in those days; and I felt that such error would never penetrate His body. How wrong I was.

In only a few years the rumbling thunder has now broken into a storm of mighty furor as more and more New Testament Christians have been swept away by the feminist winds in the world as well as by the wiles of the new hermeneutics and the smooth words of those who are intent upon changing the Lord's church. The discussions have caused some well-meaning women to question just what their roles *should* be.

There is little controversy over the traditional areas of service, such as visiting the sick and elderly as well as anyone in need of encouragement, teaching women and chil-

[10] Jane McWhorter, *She Hath Done What She Could* (Abilene, TX: Quality Publications, 1973), pp. 5-15.

dren, showing hospitality in the home, care of the building and communion preparation, sending cards, office work, and food preparation. Most of the discussions revolve around woman's part in the worship service as well as whether or not she can have authority over men in spiritual matters.

Many questions have surfaced. Were Paul's admonitions founded only upon the cultures of his time? Do they apply to women today? Women are well educated and assume roles of leadership throughout the business world. Why should their talents be stymied within the church?

Can women pray aloud when a group of men and women assemble in a home for a period of Bible study? Can they lead the Bible study under those circumstances? When a woman and her husband jointly teach a Bible-related subject to a class of men and women, is she doing wrong? Would it make any difference if that class were located in a convention center or hotel away from the church building? Could she teach such a class by herself? If a woman can read some verses of Scripture aloud from her seat at 9:30 A.M. in a Bible class discussion, why can she not stand and read those same verses aloud at the 10:30 assembly with the same men present? Can she make announcements concerning the women's activities at the beginning of the joint assembly? Can she make other announcements of general interest? If a woman can pass the communion trays from left to right while she is seated in a row, why can she not also pass them up and down the aisles from one row to another? Is this not showing a spirit of servitude? Can she lead a prayer during the public assembly? If 1 Corinthians 14 requires silence, why is she allowed to sing? If she is allowed to sing, what would be wrong with her holding a microphone in her hand and leading the women in their parts of a song before the whole assembly? How can women learn a new song without a woman to lead them? If she can lead the women during the song service, why can she not also lead the men?

If 1 Corinthians requires absolute silence, why is a woman allowed to make a public confession that Jesus is the Son of God when she is baptized? How many words is she allowed to say at this time? Is it wrong for a woman to serve on a committee in the work of the church? Can she serve on a committee which has authority over men? Can she serve as head of such a committee? If the elders give her permission to serve in a position of leadership in any sense, is she usurping authority? Isn't she usurping authority if she refuses? Can she preach in a mixed-gender assembly? Can she serve as a deacon? Was Phoebe a deacon? Can a woman be an elder? So many women were praised by Paul in Romans 16. Were they not actively involved in positions of leadership in the early days of the church? Isn't this problem within the Lord's body comparable to the race question which we faced a number of years ago? On and on the questions go.

Some believe that women should be restricted from using their natural talents in only three areas: (1) serving as elders, (2) directing the congregation's plenary assemblies during its sessions of prayer as well as (3) teaching of the Word.[11] Others teach that the only exception would be her serving as an elder.[12] Still others would not even deny her the right to be an elder.[13] Two reasons are generally cited by most feminists for restricting women: culture and flawed principles of hermeneutics.

Questioning is not wrong. Several years ago I found that searching for answers with the right attitude produced spiritual strength as I groped for reasons to my own *why*

[11] Rubel Shelly, "A Woman's Place Is . . . ," *Wineskins* 2/1 (May 1993), p. 7.

[12] Robert H. Rowland, *I Permit Not a Woman . . . to Remain Shackled* (Newport, OR: Lighthouse Publishing Co., 1991), pp. 161-162.

[13] The viewpoints of Robert M. Randolph were expressed at the Preachers' and Church Workers' Forum at Freed-Hardeman University in 1990: *Gender and Ministry* (Huntsville, AL: Publishing Designs, Inc. 1990), p. 74.

in *Let this Cup Pass*.[14] Questioning has led to an even deeper awareness of the rightful role of women in the work and worship of the church as I have personally been faced with challenges. Christians should always be willing to reexamine the Scriptures and should never accept a practice because of tradition.

Culture

The contention is made that the early restrictions were only cultural in nature. Some assert that since we are no longer living in that culture, those regulations are not binding today. While it *is* true that the Jewish women did not have the same freedom as many others around them, remember that Paul was the apostle to the Gentiles. It was common in the Greco-Roman world for women to assume leadership roles in worship. The Corinthians were certainly aware of the role of the priestesses at Delphi, the most famous center of oracles in Greece and located across the bay from Corinth. Here the one who delivered the divine oracles from the gods was a priestess. First Corinthians 14 and 1 Timothy 2 were addressed to a Hellenistic culture of people who were accustomed to hearing and seeing women in religious leadership roles. It was against this background and contrary to this culture that the restrictions were given. Christian women were to be different.[15] Since a Christian's faith is based upon the Word of God (Rom. 10:17), we must go to that Word in settling all questions. While this one chapter cannot provide an in-depth exegesis of all the pertinent passages, let us try to glean the primary biblical principles from several of them.

Galatians 3:28

Galatians 3:28 is often cited as proof that there is no distinction between the roles of men and women since the

[14] Jane McWhorter, *Let this Cup Pass* (Abilene, TX: Quality Publications, 1978).

[15] Don McWhorter, *God's Woman: Feminine or Feminist?* (Huntsville, AL: Publishing Designs, Inc., 1992), pp. 124-125.

blood of Christ has delivered us from the bondage of sin which originated in the garden.

> There is neither Jew nor Greek, there is neither bond nor free, there is neither male nor female; for ye are all one in Christ Jesus.

The blood of Christ makes us free from the law of sin and death (Rom. 8:2). Through baptism we identify with Christ's death, burial and resurrection (Rom. 6:3-4) and we become new creatures (2 Cor. 5:17).

Galatians 3:28 deals with the *worth* of Christians in God's sight, not the abolition of *roles*. There are still the roles of husbands and wives (Eph. 5:22-32), parents and children (Eph. 6:1-3), governments and citizens (Rom. 13:1-7), elders and congregations (1 Tim. 5:17; Heb. 13:17), in addition to others. While we have *different roles* to play, all Christians have the same *worth*.

Back to Creation

Different roles have been given to men and women, not because of custom and not because of the curse of sin in the garden, as a misapplication of Galatians 3:28 might lead one to believe. Instead, the matter of roles goes back to the very beginning. At the time of creation, even before the fall, God delineated various roles in spiritual matters.

In 1 Corinthians 11:3, Paul, through inspiration, wrote:

> But I would have you know, that the head of every man is Christ, and the head of the woman is the man; and the head of Christ is God.

The Greek word for head *(kephale)* means "authority, superior rank, or preeminence." In recent years feminists have insisted that the lexicons are wrong and that the real meaning of *kephale* is "source," as in "the headwater that is the source of a river."[16] (For a more detailed study of this word, the reader may consult *God's Woman: Feminine or Feminist?*).

[16] McWhorter, *God's Woman,* pp. 69-71.

From the very beginning of time, God's transcultural law stated that God is the head of Christ; Christ is the head of man; and man is the head of woman. (John 16:13-14 reveals that the Holy Spirit was also in subjection to Christ.) In the two passages which deal primarily with the roles of men and women in the church, reference is made to this original hierarchy.

(1) The reason for different spiritual roles is given in 1 Timothy 2:13: "For Adam was first formed, then Eve."

(2) First Corinthians 14 makes reference to this same normative law regarding roles in verse 34: "For it is not permitted unto them to speak; but they *are* commanded to be under obedience, as also saith the law."

To what law was Paul referring? It could not have been the Law of Moses because that law had been abolished with the death of Christ (Col. 2:14). Neither could it have referred to the law of custom because the Christians at Corinth were accustomed to seeing women who were taking a leadership role in the pagan temples. The only logical law to which it could refer would have been the law of creation, or the hierarchy of roles as given in 1 Corinthians 11:3.[17]

Christ willingly submitted to the Father, not because the Son was inferior, but because it would be best for the furtherance of the divine plan. In the same sense, woman is to submit to the leadership of her husband in the home and to male leadership in spiritual matters, not because she is inferior, but simply because it has been divinely decreed that men and women should have different roles from the very beginning of time. The *role* which each plays determines his or her *function*.

Male spiritual leadership can be found throughout the Scriptures from the very beginning of creation. It could be seen during the Patriarchal Age and was continued during the Mosaical Age. The Christian Age did away with

[17] McWhorter, *God's Woman*, pp. 96-98.

rituals of temple worship. It would have been a logical time to change the role of women in spiritual matters if it had been God's will. However, the instructions in 1 Corinthians 14 and 1 Timothy 2 continued the role of male spiritual leadership. It is the fifth chapter of Ephesians which gives an entirely new depth to the meaning of submission. Wives are to submit to their husbands, and husbands are taught that their role is one of a cherishing and loving protection, just as Christ loved and cherished the church, which is in subjection to Him.

1 Timothy 2

It is necessary to understand that the second chapter of 1 Timothy is a discussion of the *broad principle* of the role of women in the work of the church, whereas 1 Corinthians 14 is an *application* of that principle in the setting of public speaking in an assembled mixed-gender group. This distinction is important.

The theme of the entire book of 1 Timothy is given in the fifteenth verse of the third chapter: *How to Behave in the House of God*. Note that this was not a building but wherever the members had gathered in a religious setting. Often it was in a home. At other times it was in a public meeting place. Sometimes it was outside. Physical safety even necessitated assembling in the catacombs in Rome at a later time.

Stated very succinctly, the admonitions given to Timothy to pass on to the early Christians were given in order that they would know how to conduct themselves whenever and wherever they had assembled for spiritual matters.

The context for 1 Timothy 2 is male leadership in spiritual matters. In the eighth verse, Paul instructs the men *(tous andras,* from *aner)* to lead the prayers. The original word normally denotes males. It occurs 215 times in the Greek New Testament and is never translated by the word *woman* or *women* or by the phrase *men and women*. In the first verse of the same chapter, the original word for men was *anthropos,* which signified all of mankind. In other words, pray for all of mankind, both men and women. If Paul had intended to include both men and women in the leading of prayers, he would have used the Greek word *anthropos.* Instead, he used the word that is normally translated "men." The men's prayers are to come from holy lives.

In the next verse (1 Tim. 2:9) Paul begins his divinely inspired instructions for the women concerning their behavior in this same context:

> In like manner also, that women adorn themselves in modest apparel, with shamefacedness and sobriety; not with broided hair, or gold, or pearls, or costly array; but (which becometh women professing godliness) with good works (1 Tim. 2:9-10).

Some claim that those who use verses 11 and 12 of the same chapter to restrict women in spiritual matters are being inconsistent when nothing is expected concerning the dress, hairstyles, or the jewelry of modern women.

This passage is an *ellipsis,* which is a statement in which it is understood that the words *only* and *also* must be supplied. Women are to be adorned inwardly with shamefacedness and sobriety (sober mindedness). Outwardly, they are to be adorned in modest apparel, not (only) with broided hair, or gold, or pearls, or costly array; but (also) with good works. Other examples of an ellipsis are found in 1 Corinthians 1:17, John 6:27, and 1 Peter 3:3-4.

After addressing the manner in which a Christian woman is to be adorned (both inwardly and outwardly), Paul next turned his attention to her behavior in the presence of men when the group engaged in any spiritual activity. The man is to be the leader, and the woman is to learn in silence with all subjection. The word for silence in this verse *(hesuchia)* does not mean absolute silence but rather "quietness." The same root word is used in 1 Thessalonians 4:11: ". . . that ye study to be quiet," in 2 Thessalonians 3:12: ". . . that with quietness they work," in 1 Timothy 2:2: ". . . that we may lead a quiet and peaceable life," and in Acts 22:2: "And when they heard that he spake in the Hebrew tongue to them, they kept the more silence." The Christian woman submits to male spiritual leadership and learns in quietness because God has so decreed from the beginning, not because a man has told her to speak or not to speak. "But I suffer not a woman to teach, nor to usurp authority over the man, but to be in silence" (1 Tim. 2:12). *Usurp* (KJV) is not in the original text. A better translation of the Greek word *authentein* is "to have authority" (ASV, NKJV). Women are not to teach over the man or in any other way have authority over him but to be in quietness. (This kind of silence is the same that was used in verse 11.) A woman sings in the assembly and makes the confession that Jesus is the Son of God, but her role is a position of quietness. Some assert that it is all right for a woman to have a role of leadership in spiritual matters if the elders give her the authority to do so because, under those circumstances, she has not taken that authority from a man. However, no one can give authority that God has not granted.

Paul next gave the reason for woman's place of quietness and subjection in spiritual matters: *for* (because) Adam was first formed, then Eve. This reference goes back to the order of authority: God, Christ, man, woman (1 Cor. 11:3). Verse 14 gives an example of what happens when God's rule is not followed.

Dr. Carroll Osburn maintains that Paul's admonitions to the women were simply directed to a group of domineering, rude, abrasive, and misinformed women in the Ephesian church who would be teachers but still needed to be taught themselves. It was only these women who were told to be quiet. "These women had no more business teaching than Eve did. Both of them are purveyors of false information."[18] Such conjecture is merely a guess because

[18] Dr. Carroll Osburn drew these conclusions in a series of lessons on "Women in the Church," *Difficult Texts, Part 3* (Cuyahoga Falls, OH: Church of Christ, March 7-9, 1997).

there is nothing in the text to indicate such a problem. In his book, *Women in the Church,* Dr. Osburn states: "Put simply, any female who has sufficient and accurate information may teach that information in a gentle spirit to whomever in whatever situation they may be."[19]

By way of summary, whenever men and women have gathered for spiritual matters, the women are to learn in quietness, not teaching over the men or in any other way having authority over them. A woman can acceptably teach a man in a number of ways without having dominion over him. Priscilla helped her husband teach Apollos the truth (Acts 18:26), but she was not the authority figure standing before a group. A woman often quietly teaches men by appropriate comments that she may make in Bible class. However, she has never been given the right to teach in a position of authority over men. She may teach an unbelieving husband by her manner of life if he is not receptive to the Word of God (1 Pet. 3:1). This broad principle applies to the situation *anywhere* concerning spiritual matters, regardless of whether the teaching is taking place in a church building, a home, a convention hall, or in the setting of a lectureship.

1 Corinthians 14

First Corinthians 14 is an *application* of the *broad principle* that is taught in 1 Timothy 2. In previous years I personally passed over this passage as nonapplicable today because the instructions were given to those assembled at a time when miraculous gifts were being exercised. As I have matured, I have realized that this passage should not be entirely dismissed. It involves an application of the broad principle of 1 Timothy 2 (male spiritual leadership) to a specific situation (a public assembly of the church in which authoritative speaking was being done), and *that* underlying principle is still valid today.

[19] Dr. Carroll Osburn, *Women in the Church* (Abilene, TX: Restoration Perspectives, 1994), p. 115.

Verse 23 sets the tone for the entire passage under consideration. When the whole church had come together for a public assembly, certain regulations had to be followed. This chapter should be seen in context. The eleventh chapter (beginning in verse 17) teaches about the Lord's supper. The sixteenth chapter gives instructions concerning the contribution. Between these is found 1 Corinthians 14, which gives rules when public speaking is being done. The primary reason is given in verses 33 and 40: God is not the author of confusion but desires that all things be done decently and in order. Another reason is given for a woman's role. "As also saith the law" in verse 34 apparently refers to the law of creation, which determined spiritual leadership roles from the beginning: Just as God is head of Christ, man is head of woman (1 Cor. 11:3).

The word for silence *(sigao)* in this passage means "say nothing, keep silent." Whenever public speaking was being done in the assembly, sometimes the men had to be perfectly silent. Some men had the miraculous gift of an unknown tongue (the ability to speak in a foreign language that was unknown to the speaker as well as to most in the audience or sometimes even all who were present). They could speak by two or three but had to be absolutely silent if no interpreter was present. Similar rules were given to those who were exercising the gift of prophecy. Two or three could speak during an assembly, but they were admonished to take turns, speaking one at a time, and there had to be a judge to determine whether or not the prophecy was authentic.

> Let your women keep silence in the churches: for it is not permitted unto them to speak; but they are commanded to be under obedience, as also saith the law. And if they will learn any thing, let them ask their husbands at home: for it is a shame for women to speak in the church (1 Cor. 14:34-35).

When the church had assembled for worship and public speaking was being done, the women were commanded to keep silence. This silence *(sigao)* differs from the silence *(hesuchia)* which was discussed in 1 Timothy. The silence of 1 Timothy means "quietness." The silence of 1 Corinthians means "absolute silence." When the men were speaking publicly as they exercised the miraculous gifts of speaking in tongues—a foreign language—and prophesying, the women had to be absolutely silent. Some say that the term *your women* refers only to the wives of the prophets and not to women in general. Such faulty reasoning would lead to the conclusion that the single women could ask questions in the assembly but the married women could not. Others assume that Paul was only rebuking chattering women who were being disruptive. Both of these conclusions are mere speculations because the text itself is not supportive. The men sometimes had to remain silent in order for things to be done decently and in order. The women were to be silent because *the law* so decreed. The Law of Moses had already been nailed to the cross. The law of culture in the Gentile world did not prohibit women from speaking publicly at religious services. The term *the law* must refer to the law of creation.

The authenticity of these instructions was finalized in verse 37: "The things that I write unto you are the commandments of the Lord."

Eternal Principles

The second chapter of 1 Timothy involves a broad principle concerning the roles of men and women in spiritual matters. The woman must learn in a respectful quietness and in no way teach *over* the man or *have authority* over him—because of the original hierarchy of roles according to verse 13—although she certainly is free to teach a man by her example (1 Pet. 3:1) or by quietly teaching as Priscilla did (Acts 18:26).

The broad principle of 1 Timothy 2 was applied to a specific situation in 1 Corinthians 14 when the whole group had assembled and public speaking was being done. Although the men had to take turns and remain silent at times for the sake of things being done decently and in order, whenever any authoritarian roles of speaking were being exercised, the women had to remain silent (not a word) for an additional reason: "as also saith the law," the original law of roles given at the time of creation.

Now return to the questions which were considered at the beginning of this chapter. Let each one pass through four filters of ageless Bible principles that emerge from some specific problems in the early church which were addressed by Paul and which transcend the temporary exercising of spiritual gifts during the infancy of the church.

(1) A woman should respect God's plan of male spiritual leadership (1 Cor. 11:3) and learn in quietness (1 Tim. 2:11).
(2) She cannot teach *over* the man (1 Tim. 2:12).
(3) She cannot *have authority* over him in spiritual matters (1 Tim. 2:12).
(4) When the church has assembled for worship and public speaking is being done, a woman is to remain silent (1 Cor. 14:34).

The New Testament church faced cultural problems which are no longer relevant to the modern Christian. Likewise, the early Christians never encountered most of the questions which we face. Instead of giving a list of specific directives, in His wisdom God revealed divine principles which apply to all cultures in any century. Modern questions can be resolved if they *are* allowed to pass through the filters mentioned above.

Romans 16

From the reading of the sixteenth chapter of Romans, some have drawn the conclusion that the women mentioned in this passage were either leaders or co-leaders of churches which met in the homes of the early Christians. To reach such conclusions, one must read the verses through the feminists' glasses, because there is nothing in this chapter that justifies such conclusions. These women were certainly active in the work of the church just as many women are today. They were valuable helpers to Paul and others. To say that they had authority over men is unfounded and contrary to the teachings in 1 Timothy 2 and 1 Corinthians 14.

Romans 16:3 mentions Priscilla, the wife of Aquila and the one who participated with him in teaching Apollos (Acts 18:26). Nothing in the context indicates that Priscilla's part in teaching Apollos differed from the principle clearly established in Scripture concerning roles and functions based on gender.[20] (A woman may teach a man as long as she follows God's divine principles. Of course, this precludes her teaching in a public assembly.)

In Romans 16:1 Phoebe is referred to as a "servant of the church which is at Cenchrea." Although the Greek word for servant in this case is the same as the word rendered "deacon" in 1 Timothy 3:8, there is no justification for contending that she held the office of a deacon, meeting the qualifications of 1 Timothy 3:8-10.

There is nothing in the word itself or in the context that even implies that Phoebe was anything more than what all Christian women should be—a good servant in the Lord's work. This same Greek word describes the household servants who filled the waterpots at the wedding (John 2:5). It is also this same word that describes the governmental service of Nero (Rom. 13:6). Were any of these office holders in the church? In its normal and customary use, the word simply refers to one who serves. There is no justification in assigning a different meaning to the word here.[21]

[20] Don McWhorter, *God's Woman,* p. 25.
[21] Ibid.

Dave Miller's book, *Piloting the Strait*, also has an excellent discussion of the subject of deaconesses.[22]

In addition to trying to justify the leadership of women in the church through the mentioning of the women in Romans 16, feminists also use other examples. For instance, Mary Magdalene is said to have preached the first gospel sermon when she ran to tell the disciples that Christ had risen from the dead (Matt. 28:1-10). The Samaritan woman at the well is also seen in the same context. Nonsense. Telling friends about a happening is not tantamount to standing before a mixed assembly and presenting a sermon.

Woman's Unique Role

As women, we have very special roles in the work of the church. The God-given limitations placed upon us have never implied that we are inferior or second-rate citizens in the kingdom any more than Christ was inferior because of His submission to God the Father (1 Cor. 11:3). We very strongly resent any implication that the pulpit area is the only arena for the work of the church.

The wife of a young preacher was once welcomed to a new congregation by an elder's family who remarked, "We're thankful that we now have a preacher's wife who can do more than make potato salad." *All* women can do more than make potato salad or even cookies. To be perfectly honest, we are offended by any devaluation of our unique roles.

A man brings his natural strengths and weaknesses to the service of God, and a woman brings hers. She is strong in many areas in which a man is weak, and his strengths stand in sharp contrast to her weaknesses. Together, they constitute a mighty team in the kingdom.

Just as yeast works silently, but powerfully, in causing dough to rise, so does a woman's influence permeate the church as well as the community. She quietly goes about

[22] Dave Miller, *Piloting the Strait* (Pulaski, TN: Sain Publications 1996), pp. 251-254.

her work as she fulfills the physical, emotional, and spiritual needs of others that most men never seem to notice.

A woman's work begins in her heart as she enriches her life through a careful study of God's Word and as her relationship with her Lord matures. There are no limits to the heights which she can achieve spiritually.

Usually a woman is naturally gifted in the field of teaching. Because of the biblical principle in 1 Corinthians 14, she cannot assume an authoritarian role of public speaking in the assembly of the church, nor can she be the teacher of a mixed-gender Bible class, whether it is located at the church building or elsewhere (1 Tim. 2:11-12). She may teach a man on a one-to-one basis as Priscilla, by the side of her husband Aquila, taught Apollos, provided she does so with the right attitude (Acts 18:24-26). She may also teach by her manner of life (1 Pet. 3:1). More than half of the membership of the typical congregation is composed of females. If teaching adults is a woman's natural talent, her opportunities are limitless in instructing other women, whether it be teaching ladies' Bible classes, writing adult Bible class material, speaking to ladies' day meetings, or simply gathering a group of neighborhood women around her kitchen table for a weekly period of Bible study. She teaches teenage girls and introduces them to the joy of serving others. A woman with suitable qualifications can certainly be in a leadership capacity in guiding other women through various committee actions. It is usually a woman who will take the time to teach others through the avenue of grading Bible correspondence courses.

A woman seems to have a special talent in the field of teaching young children. She, more than most men, is willing to spend countless hours in preparing visual aids to enhance a lesson. It is she who will take the time to decorate a room to make it appealing to young eyes.

In the midst of the restrictions that are placed upon women in the second chapter of 1 Timothy, we are told in the tenth verse to *adorn ourselves with good works*. The golden nugget of good works glistens again in the four-teenth chapter of Mark when the woman anointed our Lord's body with ointment. He chided His followers for re-buking her for her extravagance by praising her with these words:

> . . . she hath wrought a *good work* on me . . . wheresoever this gospel shall be preached throughout the whole world, this also that she hath done shall be spoken of for a memo-rial of her (vv. 6, 9).

Not even the mighty Paul, the missionary to the Gentile world, nor Peter, the powerful speaker on the day of Pente-cost, ever received such praise.

While some assert that a woman is only fulfilling the role of a servant if she passes the communion trays to the entire congregation, the faithful woman of God feels that she does not need to assume a role of male leadership to prove her willingness to serve others. She already has more than she can possibly do in the areas of *real* service. A man may preach about a Christian's responsibilities to those who are sick; but it is the woman who usually sends cards, keeps the children, prepares food for the family, and gen-erally ministers to their needs. A man delivers the funeral address, but we women are the ones who normally reach out with a heart of compassion as we minister to those who are mourning. When hospitality is shown, we are the ones who open our homes to others, especially to newcom-ers or those who have few friends. It is a woman's eyes that normally look beneath deceiving outward layers and detect a heart that is troubled. It is those same eyes that read a letter from a grandchild to a nursing home resident who has lost her eyesight. It is her ears that patiently lis-ten as a shut-in once again tells the stories of long ago. It is her hands that minister in so many ways to needs which most men never even know exist.

In His wisdom, God has delegated to the male the role of leadership in spiritual matters, but it is the woman who uses her natural intuitive touch to fill the void of a man's cold logic. She, along with her Christian sisters, constitute a large part of the backbone of the local church as they very quietly go about their daily lives, caring for many needs that would otherwise be overlooked.

The words of this chapter are not from a man who is denying women positions of leadership. I am writing to you as a woman who has earnestly searched for answers to these questions for a number of years and who has a burning desire to do all that I can in His service to show my appreciation to God for the gift of life itself.

When feminists beckon with unscriptural enticements, may we women voice Nehemiah's words, which have echoed from the walls of time for centuries: "I am doing a great work so that I cannot come down: why should the work cease, whilst I leave it, and come down to you" (Neh. 6:3)?

We women *are* doing a great work. There are more unquestionable activities that need to be done than we can possibly accomplish in any twenty-four hour period. Why should we leave such an important role, which no one else can adequately fill, and come down? May our attitude be that of Mary: "Behold the handmaid of the Lord; be it unto me according to thy word" (Luke 1:38).

9

Moral Issues in America
Billie Hill

A desperate need today is to go back to the Bible as our standard of right and wrong. We need to return to morality as God has clearly defined it. We need to set before our young ones an example of purity and godliness.

For those of us who have been around for a number of years and watch TV and read newspapers, we can clearly see a decline of morals in America. Our homes are often crumbling right before our eyes. The divorce rate continues at an alarming rate (over one million per year). Crime is raging all around us. There are about 3,900 abortions per day. Homosexuality is on the rise. Pregnancy out of wedlock is at an all-time high. Children are being neglected and abused.

As I was watching a national talk show on TV a few nights ago, William Bennett, former Secretary of Education, was the special guest. He was relating the fact that America has always been known as a Christian nation, but we are now leading the world in the number of abortions being done, in divorce, and in crime. He stated that he was very sad about this fact and all of us should be, especially those of us who are Christians. We need to train our children in the way of righteousness. We need to teach and shape our youth in the way God would have them go. Parents need to be setting godly examples to their children, and grandparents need to be setting examples to their grandchildren.

The following startling statistics were given recently in *USA Today*.

Every Day in the USA:

2,795 teens get pregnant

1,106 teens have an abortion

6 teenagers commit suicide

372 teens miscarry

27 children die from poverty

3,288 run away from home

437 children are arrested for drinking or drunken driving

211 children are arrested for drug abuse

1,629 children are in adult jails

7,742 teenagers become sexually active

2,556 children are born out of wedlock

1,512 teenagers drop out of school

1,849 children are abused or neglected

2,989 children see their parents divorced

Homosexuality

Homosexuality is a sin. The discussion of homosexuality is not a minority right issue. It is a moral issue and we must go to the Bible to find the answer.

During the Patriarchal Age, God expressed His divine displeasure with the practice of homosexuality. In Genesis 19 we have the record of the destruction of Sodom and Gomorrah which shows beyond a doubt God's attitude toward men who would want to "know" or "have relations" with other men. Our English word *sodomy,* which Webster defines as "casual copulation in any of certain unnatural ways," is derived from this city of Sodom.

During the Mosaical Law, God expressed his displeasure with the practice of homosexuality. In Leviticus 20:13 God said, "If a man lies with a male as he lies with a woman, both of them have committed an abomination. They shall surely be put to death. Their blood shall be upon them."

In the New Testament God showed his displeasure even more vividly with homosexuality. In Romans 1, Paul through the Holy Spirit discusses the deplorable condition of the Gentile people. In verse 18, he states, "For the wrath of God is revealed from heaven against all ungodliness and unrighteousness of men, who suppress the truth in unrighteousness."

Paul describes the type of action in which these people came to be involved as "degrading passion." He names some of these actions:

> For even their women exchanged the natural use for what is against nature. Likewise also the men, leaving the natural use of the woman, burned in their lust for one another, men with men committing what is shameful, and receiving in themselves the penalty of their error which was due (Rom. 1:26-27).

The actions pointed out here are clearly homosexual practices. Paul calls them "indecent acts" and refers to the "penalty of their error."

Some people have wanted to refer to homosexuality as a sickness. Paul does not agree with that; he clearly views these acts as sin. He clearly states in Romans 1:32, "They who practice such things are worthy of death." When God so speaks, His words should not be ignored.

Homosexuality violated God's plan for the marriage relationship. Jesus said in Matthew 19:4-5:

> Have you not read that He who made them at the beginning made them male and female, and said, "For this reason a man shall leave his father and mother and be joined to his wife, and the two shall become one flesh"?

Jesus tells us that God's plan from the beginning was for one man to marry one woman.

The Bible teaches that marriage in God's sight is made up of a male and a female who become one flesh. Paul states in 1 Corinthians 7:2, "Because of sexual immorality, let each man have his own wife, and let each woman have her own husband." Many homosexuals may be living in a relationship that they see as a substitute for "traditional marriage," but it is apparent that God's view of marriage and the fulfillment of sexual desire involves one man and one woman.

Also a further statement by Paul in 1 Corinthians 6:9-10 says,

> Do you not know that the unrighteous will not inherit the kingdom of God? Do not be deceived. Neither fornicators, nor idolaters, nor adulterers, nor homosexuals, nor sodomites, nor thieves, nor covetous, nor drunkards, nor revilers, nor extortioners will inherit the kingdom of God.

The unrighteousness shall not inherit the kingdom of God or will not be able to enter into heaven. Paul numbers homosexuals among the unrighteous.

One who has been a homosexual can be saved. In 1 Corinthians 6:11, Paul says that some of the Corinthians had been involved in these very things. Some had been homosexuals, but had made a change. They had been "washed . . . sanctified . . . justified in the name of the Lord Jesus." Paul addressed some of these same people after their change in 1 Corinthians 1:2 when he said, "To the church of God which is at Corinth, to those who are sanctified in Christ Jesus, called to be saints." What power there is in the gospel!

Through the power of the gospel an unrighteous homosexual can be numbered among the saints if he is willing to give himself to God and do as God has commanded. The desire to live as a homosexual can be overcome through the help that God is able to provide through the Bible.

Homosexuality is viewed by the Bible, the Word of God, as a sin. It is morally wrong. Those who want to please Him will listen to Him and not practice such a lifestyle or condone the practice in others.

Abortion

Our country recently celebrated the twenty-fifth anniversary of the infamous *Roe v. Wade* decision which legalized abortion in America. Recent statistics show America participated in more than 36,000,000 abortions since that fateful day, January 22, 1973. The annual number of abortions has nearly doubled since *Roe v. Wade.*

There are almost 3,900 abortions per day in America. That is one every 22 seconds. For every 1,000 live births, there are 311 abortions. There are more than 145,000 second and third trimester abortions each year (*National Right to Life News*, January, 1998, pp. 4, 8, 14, 16, 18, 26).

What Does the Bible Teach on Abortion?

The word *abortion* is not specifically mentioned by that name in either the Old or the New Testament, but there are numerous divine principles that speak to the issue. Let us look at some of them.

Life is a gift from God. "He gives to all life, and breath, and all things" (Acts 17:25). As Creator and Sustainer of life, God alone has the right to take man's life (Gen. 50:15-19). Only human life is made in the image of God (Gen. 1:26). Thus, human life is elevated to a place above all forms of earthly life. This declares that man shares kinship with God. Man has always been forbidden to kill a fellow human because of the "image of God." The penalty for killing an innocent neighbor was death (Gen. 9:6).

But some say that this thing growing in the mother's womb is not human life. Some say that it is just a blob of tissue; it is not a human until it is born. Is it alive, and if so, at what point of time? It is alive when the sperm and ovum unite and conception occurs! Is it a human life? It is the product of two human lives. If it is not a human life, then what is it, animal or vegetable? Is this life merely an appendage of the mother's body? Absolutely not, since it is altogether a new life totally different from the mother. Is this human life innocent? Without a doubt! Is this human life wilfully killed in abortion? Yes, for that is the purpose of abortion. It is wrong to kill innocent human life because mankind is made in the image of God (Gen. 9:6).

Christ taught the value of human life. He taught that God so loved all the inhabitants of the earth that He gave His only Son to save them (John 3:16). He commanded that every creature in the world has an opportunity to hear the gospel and be saved (Mark 16:15-16). Little children were precious to Jesus and He rebuked those who tried to turn them away (Matt. 19:14).

No distinction is made in the Scriptures between babies in the womb and those born. The word *brephos* used to describe the baby in Elizabeth's womb is used for both prenatal and postnatal babies (Luke 1:41). It means "an unborn child, embryo, fetus; a newborn child, an infant, a babe" (*Thayer's Greek English Lexicon*, p. 105). Christians who question this should ask themselves: Was it the Christ child in Mary's womb or a lifeless blob of fetal tissue?

God's Word still teaches, "Thou shalt not kill" (Exod. 20:13, Rom. 13:9). The deliberate taking of human life without provocation or a just cause is murder. Abortion intentionally kills a human life. The abortion victim is totally innocent, having done no wrong toward the mother, her doctor, or society. There is often a selfish motive in abortion; the interests of others are placed above the baby. We are taught: "Let each of you look out not only for his own interests, but also for the interests of others" (Phil. 2:4). Unmarried couples selfishly indulge in sexual pleasure and then when pregnancy occurs, they kill the life that would embarrass them. The same attitude is seen when the married professional woman chooses to abort rather than accept the responsibility of motherhood which would hinder her personal ambition.

God condemns people who are "without natural affection" (Rom. 1:31). Without a doubt, a mother that can deliberately kill the innocent child in her womb lacks that normal, motherly affection which God expects from mankind.

Objections Considered

Some people argue that since Adam did not become alive until God breathed into him the breath of life and the baby does not draw breath until he leaves the womb, the unborn baby has no soul and thus can be killed without guilt. This is not a parallel since Adam had no life at all until God gave him life. But a baby from the moment of conception is alive and growing. His oxygen is supplied through his umbilical cord which is attached to the mother. He replaces that at birth with another system more suited to his new environment. James says the body apart from the spirit is dead (James 2:26). It is a biological fact that human life begins at conception.

Some feel that the unborn child is of less value than the mother; therefore, she has a right to kill it if it bothers her. The passage used to try to prove this is Exodus 21:22-23:

> If men fight, and hurt a woman with child, so that she gives birth prematurely, yet no lasting harm follows, he shall surely be punished accordingly as the woman's husband imposes on him; and he shall pay as the judges determine. But if any lasting harm follows, then you shall give life for life.

Their reasoning is that "if the baby is killed, only a fine is imposed, but if the mother is killed, capital punishment is given. Therefore, unborn babies are not persons." This cannot be the case because verses 28-37 of Exodus 21 state if a man's ox gores a free man, the animal and the owner shall be put to death, but if it only gores a servant (alone), the owner of the ox shall pay a fine. Since the slave's death is punished less than the free man's, do we conclude that slaves are not full persons and can be killed without impunity? If the case of the woman and her unborn baby teaches that the baby's life is less valuable, then this conclusion about slaves also follows.

The words "and yet no harm follows" may mean the child is miscarried but does not die. Then the expression "if any harm follows" means that if either the child, the mother, or both die, then the guilty party is to be punished with death. If this be the case then no greater value is placed on the adult than the prenatal life. The fine is for the injury which caused the early delivery; the death penalty is for the causing of a death of either mother or child. Regardless of the construction we put in the passage, it does not parallel the abortion situation. Moses is dealing with accidental damage to the mother or child. In abortion, a deliberate decision is made by the mother and doctor to destroy the living baby in the womb.

Can we kill the baby if the mother's life is threatened? A doctor's mission is to save life, not to kill it. Some are faced with a truly "either/or" situation. A doctor may remove a cancerous uterus or a tubal pregnancy. In doing this, the child would inadvertently die. But this was not the purpose of the surgery. The purpose was to save a dying mother. This is a fine distinction that reflects a difference in nature and a sacred respect for all human life. Situations where the mother's life is at stake because of the pregnancy are very rare today.

If the baby is a result of rape, can we abort it? We must be very sympathetic to victims of rape and must help them every way that we can. Statistics show that less than one percent of our annual million-and-a-half abortions are for rape, deformity, incest, and threat to the mother's life. Judges have declared the death penalty for rapists to be cruel and inhumane. The guilty father gets a few years in prison and sometimes goes free. But the innocent little baby in the womb gets capital punishment. He has done nothing wrong in the case. Is this fair?

If there is a danger of deformity, could we then abort the baby? Is all human life sacred, or just some? Is the defective baby in the womb human? If we can abort the defective unborn, why not kill the defective at birth? What is the difference? Should we decide to eliminate those who are imperfect? If so, just how perfect will one have to be before he is allowed to live? Who will have the power to make the decision? Does any man have the wisdom or the right to play God? Many times I have had parents tell me that the doctor told them their child was deformed and they should have an abortion, and they were delighted to show off their beautiful, normal child that they chose to have by ignoring the doctor's advice.

Some argue that it is more merciful to abort a baby than to bring it into the world where there are bad circumstances, especially poverty. This was the argument made to me by some college girls in Moscow when I was teaching their sociology class. I was asked by their regular teacher to come speak to their class on the Women's Liberation Movement in America. I said I would be glad to do this if I could also talk about abortion. I found out while there that Russia put pregnant girls who wanted an abortion in the hospital and performed it and the government paid for it. Some of the girls in my class got very upset at the things I was teaching. They argued that it was more merciful to abort a baby than to bring it into a situation as their country was in at the time with such extreme poverty. I felt at the time by the reaction of some of these girls that they probably had already had an abortion.

Kinds of Abortions Being Done

1. Partial-Birth Abortion
   This procedure is used after twenty weeks (four-and-a-half months) of pregnancy and often to six, seven, eight, and even nine months. Guided by ultrasound, the abortionist grabs the baby's legs. The baby's legs are pulled out into the birth canal. The abortionist jams scissors into the baby's skull. The scissors are then opened to enlarge the hole. A suction tube is in-

serted. The child's brains are sucked out, causing the skull to collapse. The dead baby is then removed.

The anesthesia given to the mother has little or no effect on the baby according to congressional testimony by the nation's leading anesthesiologist, including the president of the American Society of Anesthesiologists. Medical experts testified that babies at this age can experience great pain.

Dr. Martin Haskill, who has performed over a thousand partial-birth abortions, said that he performs them "routinely" for nonmedical reasons, and that eighty percent are "purely elective." Over three hundred leading physicians, including former U.S. Surgeon General C. Everett Koop, have stated that partial-birth abortion is never medically necessary to protect a mother's health.

Congress passed an act to end partial-birth abortion except to save the life of the mother. President Clinton vetoed the act, thereby allowing this brutal procedure to continue with no restrictions.

2. Suction Curettage
   This procedure is used from one to three months and eighty percent of all abortions are done by this method. It is only a fifteen-minute procedure. It is done by dilation with dilator rods. A powerful suction tube is inserted through the cervix into the womb. The developing baby's body and placenta are torn into pieces and sucked into a jar. The head is crushed and extracted.

3. Dilation and Evacuation (D&E)
   This procedure takes place from four to eight months. The cervix is dilated using laminaria (seaweed) and dilator rods. Forceps are inserted inside, grasping body parts, twisting them off, and removing them in pieces. The spine and skull are crushed and extracted. A curette (sharp, oval-shaped knife) is used to scrape

out the uterus. Baby pieces are reassembled to verify completion.

4. Salt Poisoning or Saline Method
   This procedure is done from four to seven months. A long needle is inserted into the mother's abdomen and a strong salt solution is injected directly into the amniotic fluid surrounding the baby. Salt is swallowed and "breathed," slowly poisoning the baby and severely burning its skin. The mother goes into labor within twenty-four hours and expels the dead and shriveled baby. Some babies survive "salting out" and are born with severe complications.

5. Prostaglandin
   This type of abortion is done from four to eight months. The Upjohn Company of Kalamazoo, Michigan developed and sells these hormone-like compounds. They are injected or applied to uterine muscles, causing intense contractions, expelling the developing baby. There are often side effects, and live births are common. The testing of self-administered tampons of chemicals are widely promoted in India, China, and Eastern Europe.

6. Digoxin Induction
   This type of abortion is done from five to eight months. The cervix is dilated as in a D&E. Ultrasound imaging is used to guide a syringe filled with digoxin (adult heart monitoring drug) into the heart of the baby, stopping it instantly. Prostaglandin induces labor, which delivers a dead baby. This one is virtually a hundred percent effective.

7. Hysterotomy or Cesarean Section
   This is usually done from four to eight months. An incision is made through the abdomen into the womb. The baby is removed and allowed to die by neglect, or is killed by strangulation or some other direct act while still inside the mother.

8. RU 486 (Morning-After Pill)
   This one began its use in Europe. This produces bad
   cramping and bad side effects. It is used in conjunc-
   tion with prostaglandin (Bergel & Koop, M.D., *Abortion in America*, 1990).

Abortion Involves Risks, Trauma, and Side Effects

Because induced abortion is an unnatural, hostile pen-
etrating of a closed and safeguarded biological system—
the child in the womb—the mother is always exposed to
risks and to short and long-term complications, both physical and psychological.

Incomplete abortion resulting in blood clotting, bleed-
ing, hemorrhage, and infections are not uncommon. Men-
strual disturbances, miscarriage, tubal pregnancies, and
sterility are always risks and tend to multiply with suc-
cessive abortions.

Cervical lacerations and uterine perforation can result
from suction and D&E procedures. Convulsions, severe
vomiting, and diarrhea are commonplace with prostaglandin abortions. Cardiac arrests and maternal deaths have
also been reported.

Long-term psychological effects, which are just now beginning to be seriously studied include guilt, anxiety, depression, anger, sense of loss, nightmares, distortion of self-
image, and even suicide.

Like the veterans of war, veterans of abortion attempt
to cope with their hidden trauma by denial and suppres-
sion, and so fail to acknowledge their grief for those who
did not survive. In the case of the women the loss is greater;
the dead is her own unborn child, and she finds herself
helplessly re-experiencing the death scene in recurring
dreams and intrusive memories, even years later. Reaction on the anniversary of the abortion or the expected
birth date of the child is particularly intense.

Not only are the mothers of aborted unborn suffering,
but fathers, surviving siblings, grandparents, and abortion

providers are also experiencing negative psychological consequences as well. Fathers of the unborn in particular have been legally and psychologically ignored both in the abortion decision and its aftermath. These "forgotten fathers" often suffer the trauma of abortion as intensively as the female partners.

Abortion Is Shedding Innocent Blood

In Proverbs 6:16-17, Solomon the wise man says, "These six things the Lord hates, yea, seven are an abomination to Him: a proud look, a lying tongue, hands that shed innocent blood."

In comparison to the 3,900 children that are killed each day in America or the several million abortions that will be performed this year throughout the world, Pharaoh's extermination of the Hebrew boys was but a ripple on the ocean of time. The slaughter of the babies in Bethlehem by Herod did not equal one abortion clinic's daily quota.

Many believe that the Vietnam War was one of the most senseless, useless, and unraveling wars in our nation's history. Because of this war, the United States has received much criticism and very bad publicity. There is a war that has been forgotten. This war was declared January 22, 1973, by our Supreme Court. This war is waged daily in hospitals, doctors' offices, and medical centers throughout our land. It is the war on the unborn. Notice the following gruesome facts from July 1987 *National Federation of Decency Journal:*

U.S. War Dead

Revolutionary War	25,324
War of 1812	2,260
Mexican War	13,283
Civil War	498,332
Spanish American War	2, 446
World War I	116,708
World War II	407,316

Korean War	54,246
War on the Unborn	36,000,000

This means that there have been 32 times as many deaths by legalized abortion than the 1,119,915 Americans killed in armed conflict since the founding of our nation.

Living Together before Marriage Is a Sin

Living together outside of marriage violates God's way. God calls it fornication and Christians are admonished to "abstain from sexual immorality" (Acts 15:20), to "flee sexual immorality" (1 Cor. 6:18) and to "avoid sexual immorality" (1 Cor. 7:2). Paul declares, "Flee sexual immorality. Every sin that a man does is outside the body, but he who commits sexual immorality sins against his own body" (1 Cor. 6:18). Fornication is described as a work of the flesh (Gal. 5:19) and the warning is given to "let it not even be named among you, as is fitting for saints" (Eph. 5:3). Christians are exhorted not to eat with a Christian brother who is a fornicator (1 Cor. 5:11). Those guilty of fornication should repent (2 Cor. 12:21) and those who do not "shall not inherit the kingdom of God" (1 Cor. 6:9).

An article called "Cohabitation Won't Ensure Marital Bliss" appeared in the *Tennessean* (July 30, 1989). This article stated that certain researchers who expected the widespread practice of "trial marriage" to bring in an era of increased martial stability have been surprised by the studies.

For several years the number of couples who live together before marriage has been increasing. Some thought the practice would promote more successful marriages. However, a recent survey showed that the practice had a detrimental effect on marriage, not a positive one.

A 1987-1988 federally funded survey of 13,000 people attests to the failure of their practice to build strong marriages. *The National Survey of Family and Households* shows that within ten years of their wedding, thirty-eight percent of those who had lived together before marriage split up as compared to twenty-seven percent of those who simply married.

The practice continues to increase at an alarming rate. The number of people who live together before marriage continues to climb, especially for people who marry more than once; sixty percent of those who remarried between 1980 and 1987 set up housekeeping with someone, usually the eventual spouse, beforehand.

I am sure more recent studies would show this number even higher. This practice still seems to be on the increase. This type of living is what has led to the increased number of abortions in our country. Most abortions occur as a result of sex outside of wedlock.

God's children must strive to live lives influenced by God and not by the world. We must work to instill in Christians, especially our youth, that our moral standards must be set by God and not by the world. Worldly influences around us are tremendous. Paul tells us, "And do not be conformed to this world, but be transformed by the renewing of your mind, that ye may prove what is that good and acceptable and perfect will of God" (Rom. 12:2).

God's way always proves to be the best way. Living together before marriage may be the popular way of the world, but it is not God's way and it will not produce better marriages. It will without a doubt bring about many more abortions.

10

What Can I Do about False Teaching?
Debbie Kea

The devil is hard at work. He is out to get the church. He already has the world; no need to worry about them. He wants us—the Lord's church. One of the ways he accomplishes this is by taking the Word of God away from us. Why does he bother to do this? Because he knows the Word is the only thing that can save us.

Snatching the Word of God from people has become an easy task of late. The adversary has taken advantage of a dangerous climate that has developed. Brethren have become lazy and thus ignorant when it comes to knowing the Scriptures. Add to ignorance a lack of respect and you have the perfect opportunity for Satan's ministers to slip in and attempt to replace God's Word with false doctrine.

False doctrines come in every size, shape, and color, so we cannot consider them all, but there are a few that seem to be the devil's current favorites:

> Change agents in the church
> Grace only
> The role of women
> Christians in all churches
> Setting aside of authority

Change Agents in the Church

It appears many in the church think change is the answer to their every problem, but not by changing their lives to conform to God's will. No, that's not what they want to change. They want to change God's plan, God's pattern. Every time I hear of a Christian or congregation that's ventured from the truth, I am still amazed. How arrogant and presumptuous can folks be? Every time someone changed God's plan in the Old Testament, he was punished. Every time! I'm reminded of Saul in 1 Samuel 13. He offered a burnt offering. He acted as a priest when it wasn't his place. Samuel told him, "Thou hast done foolishly: thou hast not kept the commandment of the Lord " (v. 13). Saul took it upon himself to change God's commanded way. I know brethren who would be taking up for Saul at this point. They have to, when you consider the changes they've implemented in the church. Praying, giving, remembering Jesus' death, singing, and listening to God's Word aren't good enough anymore for some brethren. Instead they embrace the doctrines of men and thus render their worship vain (Matt. 15:9). The change agents in the church would have us believe you can't be spiritual and sound. I know it's possible. In fact, that's what God has always expected—doing the right thing in the right way from the right heart (John 4:24).

Grace Only

This is another popular yet absurd doctrine. If grace were all salvation took, wouldn't every single person be saved, since God wants everyone to be saved (2 Pet. 3:9)? Of course we can't do anything to earn or ever deserve to be saved. Jesus has given the one thing to pay our debt— His blood. But if we do not respond in loving obedience, what good is His gift? Jesus said, "He that *doeth* the will of my Father" would enter heaven (Matt. 7:21). I believe Jesus. I must *do*. I must act. Peter told those at Pentecost to "save yourselves from this untoward generation" (Acts 2:40). We must act. We work out our own salvation (Phil. 2:12) according to Paul, we are blessed when we keep God's Word (Luke 11:28) according to Jesus, and we are blessed and have a right to the tree of life when we *do* His commandments (Rev. 22:14) according to John. God help us to so do.

Role of Women

It is clear by reading 1 Timothy 2:8-13 that God intends for women to be restricted in certain activities. Those that deny this must turn a deaf ear to plain Scripture. God's Word does not allow women to lead singing, pray, or teach in a mixed group. It's just that easy to understand. First Corinthians 11:1-3 explains that man is the head of woman. But some today argue this was a cultural tradition, that God didn't intend this to be an eternal plan. However, Paul made it clear when he went all the way back to Genesis 3 to make his point in 1 Timothy 2. The principle of headship goes back to creation.

I remember reading an article by a so-called enlightened woman a few years back in which she claimed that the church was stifling women, that women were being relegated to fixing potluck meals when they had so many other talents. They were making decisions daily in the work world for big corporations, running businesses, and so on, yet in the church were only allowed to do the menial. I recall being highly insulted by this woman's attitude. I still am. She came very close to blaspheming God as far as I'm concerned. She is questioning God's plan. She is also implying that Christian women as servants in the kingdom are unimportant and play an insignificant role. I strongly disagree! Jesus said a cup of water given in His name would cause one to receive a blessing. The truth of the matter is we have too many women who want the limelight, who want to be running the show instead of serving in the show! It is the servant that Jesus said would be great in the kingdom, not the CEO. I see a lack of humility on the part of many women today who do not understand their roles as servant and helpmeet. We have to be seeking the praise of our Father, not the applause of men (or women).

Christians in All Churches

The truth that you must be in the body of Christ to be a Christian seems to have become a "hard saying" for some brethren of late. Christians in all churches (they mean denominations) is now the liberal cry. This absurd false doctrine (have you noticed how these false doctrines are so absurd when placed side by side with truth?) is one that many embrace as a matter of convenience. Isn't it so much easier to just accept everyone and never question them? After all, we all believe in Jesus, don't we? Christianity never has been a matter of convenience. It is a choice for what is right, no matter what subject or what level you are on. Acts 2:47 says, "And the Lord added to the church daily such as should be saved." Acts 20:28 teaches that the Lord purchased the church with His own blood. So those who are saved, bought with His blood, are in His church. Jesus is the Savior of the body, His church, and we are baptized into that body (Eph. 1:22-23; 5:23; Gal. 3:27). If we have believed and obeyed the truth, then we are in that body and among the believers. We cannot believe error and obey truth. How pure and simple is the gospel!

Setting Aside of Authority

All of the popular false doctrines have come about because of this one—the setting aside of the authority of God. Only when mankind bows to the Almighty Creator can we be pleasing to Him. Colossians 3:17 is explicit: "And whatsoever ye do in word or deed, do all in the name of the Lord Jesus, giving thanks to God and the Father by him." Speaking where God speaks and being silent where He is silent is a scriptural concept: "If any man speak, let him speak as the oracles of God" (1 Pet. 4:11). Many brethren have become impressed by each other instead of by God. They think more of themselves than they should (1 Cor. 4:6; Gal. 6:3). These folks have forgotten the words of Jesus: "He that rejecteth me, and receiveth not my words, hath one that judgeth him: the word that I have spoken, the same shall judge him in the last day" (John 12:48). There is only one way we can honor Jesus—by doing what He says.

Now, what can I, as a woman, do about these problems?

1. *Study.* I must prepare myself. I must believe the truth and be ready to give an answer (1 Pet. 3:15).

2. *Pray.* I should pray for the body of Christ and for strength.

3. *Take a Stand.* I must "be strong in the Lord." There are too many who need to get a backbone.

4. *Be Supportive.* I should encourage sound men everywhere who teach and preach the truth.

5. *Teach.* I should teach my children at home about the Lord and His Way, about His church, and His plan of salvation. If I teach a Bible class, I should endeavor to impress upon them the truth about Jesus' one church, how God wants us to worship Him, and other basic truths. Finally, I can and should teach those with whom I come in contact.

6. *Be Informed.* I can't help fight if I don't know about the war. If I know what's going on, I can be prepared and be an influence for good. I should secure good material that exposes error and make it available to others as well.

7. *Honor the Lord.* There is only one way we honor Jesus—that's by doing what He says. We must live the truth that we defend. Only then do we honor our Lord (John 14:15; 15:14).

These are general suggestions that should be engaged in continually. But what should we do if we see or hear false doctrine in our own congregation?

If you are married to a faithful Christian, you should discuss the error with your husband. You should take a stand together for the truth by going to the elders. If the elders handle it, you've helped solve the problem. If the elders do not handle it, then you and your husband will have to decide if there's anything else you can do and how long you can stay with this congregation without compromising the truth. If it is clearly false doctrine, you must uphold your husband as he tries to warn the brethren and expose the error. This could be very difficult because of relatives and close friends in the congregation. So you must therefore make a prior commitment that you will not compromise.

Someone might ask, "What if I'm sitting in a class and hear, or my children come home from a Bible class having heard, false doctrine? Do I go to the teacher or the elders?" You can go to both but you must go to the elders. Why not just the teacher?

The elders are held responsible for the public teaching and preaching done in the church. A class is public. To properly shepherd the flock, the elders must know what is being taught and that it is the truth.

If you do not have a faithful Christian husband, you can go to the elders yourself, or if you feel more comfortable, talk to a brother in Christ whom you trust and take him with you. Either way your concerns need to be voiced. Just because you're single doesn't mean you have no responsibility to the truth or the church.

Finally

There will always be false teachers (2 Pet. 2:1), and many will follow them (2 Pet. 2:2). It was true in the first century; it is true today. We must be ready to recognize them and stand against them. When we see teachers who reject God's authority (Jude 8), who resist the truth (2 Tim. 3:8), who are deceitful (Eph.4:14) and depart from the faith (1 Tim. 4: 1-2), and when we see those who have forsaken the right way (2 Pet. 2:15), we must take the proper steps toward them, for our souls and for theirs. It is vital that we maintain a proper Christian attitude (James 5:19-20; Gal. 6:1). If possible, see that they are taught accurately God's Word (1 Tim. 2:4; Acts 18:24-28; Jude 22). They must be brought to their senses (2 Tim. 3:7; Titus 2:1-6). Through it all we must be patient, humble and gentle (2 Tim. 2:24-26), even after we have seen them warned a first and second time, rebuked sharply, and finally brought before the church (Titus 1:13; 3:9-10; Jude 22-23).

Those who do not repent must be avoided and delivered to Satan (1 Tim. 1:18-20; 1 Cor. 5:4-5; Rom. 16:17). It is difficult and heartbreaking and takes much strength but we cannot share in their evil deeds (2 John 9-11).

God help us to believe the truth, obey it, teach it and defend it!

11

The ChristianWoman's Tongue
Billie Hill

"Let no corrupt communication proceed out of your mouth, but what is good for necessary edification, that it may impart grace to the hearers" (Eph. 4:29).

It seems that most people think that women are plagued the most with sins of the tongue. This issue may be debatable but nevertheless as Christian women we need to know how to control our tongue. James tells us in James 1:26 that if we do not bridle our tongue, our religion is vain. This inspired writer had a great deal to say about our speech and our use of words. We need to study very seriously his admonition.

Though the tongue cannot be tamed, it must be controlled. We never get too old that we do not have to control or watch our tongue lest it harm or destroy. It can never be given free rein.

I have met a few older people who seemed to think that because they were older, they could say what they pleased regardless of who it might hurt. This is not God's will. Let us consider some of the ways that we can sin with our tongue.

1. *Gossip:* Talebearing has always been a plague to society. God stated, "You shall not go about as a talebearer among your people" (Lev. 19:16). "A talebearer reveals

secrets, but he who is of a faithful spirit conceals a matter" (Prov. 11:13). It is never wise to tell secrets. A faithful friend keeps a secret but a talebearer reveals it. He is not saying here that "a talebearer is one who is telling lies." Many things that are true should never be repeated and here God is condemning "tattlers" as speaking things they ought not. Some people seem to delight in hearing and telling the most corrupt things. Beware of the person who goes around prefacing his statements with: "Keep this to yourself, but have you heard . . ."; "They tell me . . ."; "I'll tell you something if you won't tell anyone . . ."; or "I can't believe this but . . ."

God said in the long ago that the righteous are not to associate with this kind of people. "He who goes about as a talebearer reveals secrets; therefore do not associate with one who flatters with his lips" (Prov. 20:19). If we have an eagerness to hear evil and slander, we reveal that we have a wicked heart. Solomon said, "An evildoer gives heed to false lips; a liar listens eagerly to a spiteful tongue" (Prov. 17:4).

Three Golden Gates

If you are tempted to reveal
A tale someone has told
About another make it pass,
Before you speak, three narrow gates of gold.

These narrow gates: First, "Is it true?"
Then "Is it needful?"
In your mind
Give truthful answer,
And the next
Is narrowest: "Is it kind?"

And if to reach the lips at last,
It passes through the gateways three;
Then you may tell the tale
Nor fear what the results may be.
                                    Author Unknown

Gossip is forbidden by God. God spoke of some women as being "idle, wandering about from house to house; and not only idle but also gossips and busybodies, saying things which they ought not" (1 Tim. 5:13).

"Even so the tongue is a little member and boasts great things. See how great a forest a little fire kindles! And the tongue is a fire, a world of iniquity" (James 3:5-6). The church has some agitators who enjoy starting a fire and then watching it become a huge blaze.

Gossip can separate friends, promote strife, wreck homes and families, and destroy the influence of the church in communities. Gossip is contrary to every Christian principle. If there were no gossipy ears, there would soon be no gossipy tongues.

Gossip is one form of slander. A slanderer is one who utters false reports or tales with the intent to injure the reputation of another.

A Christian woman will not let her words be hurtful to others. Once a word is said it cannot be "unsaid."

The late B. C. Goodpasture had a favorite saying which I heard him say many times: "The less you say, the less you have to take back." Brother Goodpasture was my mother's first cousin and I was around him from childhood. I worked for him at the Gospel Advocate when I was a student at David Lipscomb College. His dear wife Freddie presented my husband and me a beautiful cross-stitched version of this saying which she had made a few years back. It now hangs in my living room and I never read it without it making an impression on me to watch my words.

A careless word may kindle strife;
A cruel word may wreck a life.
A bitter word may hate instill
A brutal word may smite and kill.

A gracious word may smooth the way;
A joyous word may light the way;
A timely word may lessen stress;
A loving word may heal and bless.
                    Author Unknown

2. *Lying:* Lying has become a very prevalent thing in society today. Satan is the father of all lies (John 8:44) and all liars will spend eternity with him (Rev. 21:8). God said in Proverbs 6:16-19 that one of the things that He hates the most is lying.

Many children learn to lie because they hear their parents lie. Many parents will tell a child to answer the door or the telephone and to tell the person that they are not there. How can they later punish the same child for lying about some other matter when they have set such a bad example?

It is a sad commentary on our nation when prominent political leaders set such bad examples by lying before our young people. A person who lies is like Satan for "he is a liar and the father of it" (John 8:44). The doom for liars is: "Their part shall be in the lake that burneth with fire and brimstone; which is the second death" (Rev. 21:8). All Christians must tell the truth. Paul said in Ephesians 4:25, "Therefore putting away lying, each one speak truth with his neighbor."

Beware of the Devil's Daughters:

Miss Information
Miss Interpretation
Miss Representation
Miss Conception
Miss Construction
Miss Understanding
These are dangerous girls!! Beware!!
                    Author Unknown

3. *Anger and Uncontrolled Temper:* "Be angry, and do not sin: do not let the sun go down on your wrath"

(Eph. 4:26). Anger is sometimes justifiable, but we must watch lest it lead us to sin. If we cannot control ourselves, we cannot guide others. Proverbs 25:28 states, "Whoever has no rule over his own spirit is like a city broken down without walls." "A soft answer turns away wrath, but a harsh word stirs up anger" (Prov. 15:1). It is not wise for one always to speak his mind; God says he is a fool if he does. Some people boast and say, "I say what I think," not knowing that they are foolish. God says: "A fool vents all his feelings, but a wise man holds them back" (Prov. 29:11). Christians are not to be contentious but gentle (Titus 3:2).

> Angry words! O let them never
>   from the tongue unbridled slip;
> May the heart's best impulse ever
>   check them ere they soil the lip.

4. *Filthy Language:* "But now you must also put off all these: anger, wrath, malice, blasphemy, filthy language out of your mouth" (Col. 3:8).

When filthy language comes out of the mouth this shows that we have a filthy heart, "for out of the abundance of the heart the mouth speaks" (Matt. 12:34). As Christians our conversation should be pure. We should not tell dirty jokes nor should we laugh when others are telling them. As Christians we must think on things that are pure (Phil. 4:8). We should always season our speech with salt (Col. 4:6).

Closely related to filthy speaking is taking God's name in vain or using bywords. "You shall not take the name of the Lord your God in vain" (Exod. 20:7). This command tells us not to use God's name in any irreverent or disrespectful way. There are many things worthy of respect and honor. We honor our parents and we would not want anyone to speak of them in a disrespectful manner. We respect our flag and it upsets us greatly when men treat it in a light way. How much more should we respect the name of the Lord our God (Heb. 12:28)?

It is most regrettable that there is so much disrespect for the name of God in our nation. So many people take God's name in vain so very thoughtlessly. "The Lord will not hold him guiltless that takes his name in vain" (Exod. 20:7). "Out of the same mouth proceed blessing and cursing. My brethren, these things ought not to be so" (James 3:10). "But above all, my brethren, do not swear, either by heaven or by earth or with any other oath. But let your 'yes' be 'yes' and your 'no,' 'no,' lest you fall into judgment" (James 5:12).

Many who would not think of cursing will use bywords which are very closely akin. It reflects upon our intelligence when we take God's name in vain or use bywords. It shows that since there are about 400,000 words in the English language, we do not have the ability to express ourselves without showing irreverence for God.

The wives of elders, deacons, and preachers need to be especially careful in their speech. The wives of elders and deacons have many opportunities to come in contact with many people because of the work of their husbands. Because of these contacts, her example and influence as a Christian may be widely felt. First Timothy 3:11 states, "Likewise their wives must be reverent, not slanderers, temperate, faithful in all things." This Scripture is sandwiched between the characteristics laid out for elders and deacons. This Scripture should not be pointed to as traits to qualify them for an official position, because all women, as Christians, are instructed to be "grave, not slanderers, sober and faithful in all things." These traits are especially needful to the wives of elders and deacons. The lack of these traits, as well as some others in his wife, can seriously handicap the elder or deacon in the performance of his duties.

In my forty-two years as a preacher's wife, and some of those years as an elder's wife, I have seen a number of problems brought on by wives who did not control their tongues as they should have. I remember one situation where an elders' meeting was conducted and some serious matters were being discussed pertaining to future leadership of that congregation. After that meeting one elder went home and told his wife some of the statements that had been made at that meeting. The elder's wife immediately got on the phone and called a deacon's wife, who got on the phone and called almost every woman in the congregation by the next day. Needless to say, this caused much trouble in the church which lingered for years. This certainly proved that these two women were not qualified to be the wives of an elder or deacon.

The wife of an elder or deacon should hold her tongue and her temper. She should be careful about becoming involved in arguments and should avoid making rash and extreme statements. She should be a woman who uses good sense. Also, wives of preachers and women who are Bible school teachers should possess more than just a minimum amount of qualities of good character.

5. *Double-Tongued:* One of the negative qualifications of deacons is "not double-tongued" (1 Tim. 3:8). So many people have double tongues (Ps. 50:19). They talk one way to your face and they talk another way when your back is turned. "Their tongue is an arrow shot out; it speaks deceit; one speaks peaceably to his neighbor with his mouth, but in his heart he lies in wait" (Jer. 9:8). As Christians it is our duty to speak in such a way that people can believe what we say, knowing that we will always speak the truth.

6. *False Teaching:* "There are some that would trouble you, and would pervert the gospel of Christ" (Gal. 1:7). Christ warned of wolves in sheep's clothing (Matt. 7:15). Peter said in 2 Peter 2:1-3 that just as there had been false prophets among the people, there would also be false teachers who would make merchandise of souls. There were some who were "teaching things which they ought not, for filthy lucre's sake" (Titus 1:11). Man cannot change God's Word (Deut. 4:2; Rev. 22:18-19). We should make sure that we are always teaching the truth. Teaching and preaching the Word of God is a great responsibility. James said, "Let not many of you become teachers, knowing that we shall receive a stricter judgment" (James 3:1).

God wants us as His children to be very careful about the things we say. Proverbs 29:20 says, "Do you see a man who is hasty in his words? There is more hope for a fool than for him." Matthew 12:36-37 says,

> But I say to you that for every idle word men may speak, they will give an account of it in the day of judgment. For by your words you will be justified, and by your words you will be condemned.

> The tongue of the righteous is choice silver (Prov. 10:20).

> A word fitly spoken is like apples of gold in settings of silver (Prov. 25:11).

We must keep in mind that the Lord knows the way we speak. We must give an account of our words.

I Am Your Tongue

I am your tongue! I am small and pink. One end is fastened, the other end goes wag, wag, wag! The Bible mentions me about 215 times. Read Proverbs 18:21 and 21:23 to see what an important fellow I am.

When I say kind words, thoughtful words, true words, it makes other people happy and it makes you happy. When

I say mean words, angry words, whining words, untrue words, there is trouble for other people and trouble for you.

You cannot say a word without me, but I never say a word without orders from you. You are the boss. When you have hurt someone, you try to excuse yourself by saying, "Oh, that was just a slip of the tongue. I didn't mean it." Well, boss, don't pin the blame on me. The slip was further back along the line in your thoughts and in your feelings. The things you don't mean to speak have a meaning all the same. Your tongue gives away the secrets of your heart. Jesus understood this very well, for He said,

> For out of the abundance of the heart the mouth speaks. A good man out of the good treasure of his heart brings forth good things, and an evil man out of the evil treasure brings forth evil things . . . For by your words you will be justified, and by your words you will be condemned (Matt. 12:34-37).

There is no such thing as a "slip of the tongue" for the tongue speaks only what it is commanded to speak. "If anyone among you thinks he is religious, and does not bridle his tongue but deceives his own heart, this one's religion is useless" (James 1:26).

"Even so the tongue is a little member and boasts great things. See how great a forest a little fire kindles!" (James 3:5).

> With it we bless our God and Father, and with it we curse men, who have been made in the similitude of God. Out of the same mouth proceed blessing and cursing. My brethren, these things ought not so to be (James 3:9-10).

Author Unknown
Ypsilanti, Michigan church bulletin

PART FIVE

Special Areas

12

A Missionary's Wife
Bonnie Ruiz

A missionary's wife: Is she special? Sacrificial? Understanding and forgiving? Is she compassionate, optimistic, and adventurous? Does she have a sense of humor? Must she be bold and responsible? Should she love to teach? Does she have to be a strong Christian example and hospitable? Does she have to love her husband with all her heart?

Yes, I believe every one of these traits will help her in her service to God on the mission field. Let us ponder together each of these characteristics and see how they will help her in her daily life in a faraway land, or in a place where the church is weak or nonexistent.

Is the missionary wife special? Yes, she is very special—just as all children of God are very special in His sight. We are so precious in God's sight that He sent His only begotten Son into the world to die a felon's death for our sins (John 3:16). Jesus purchased the church with His own blood (Acts 20:28). "Greater love hath no man than this, that a man lay down his life for his friends" (John 15:13).

Do you not feel special when you dwell on God's love for you? The missionary wife does. When her husband feels the responsibility to preach the gospel beyond the sea, she does not begin to think of all the reasons they cannot go. The children are too small. I can't leave my parents. We'll never raise so much support. I don't want to leave my house—I just got it the way I want it. There are others more experienced—let them go; besides, there isn't a Wal-Mart! (Yes, I really had someone say that to me.) No, she remembers God's great sacrifice for her and says, "Here I am Lord, send me."

It seems in talking to women about taking the gospel beyond the sea that their biggest barrier is not wanting to sacrifice. Yes, every missionary wife will have to sacrifice. Praise God for the greater opportunity the missionary wife has to grow in this very important Christian virtue. With sacrificing comes suffering, whether it be physical, emotional, or spiritual. When we think of the greatest sacrifice and the greatest suffering, of whom do we think? Is it not our Lord Himself?

"Looking unto Jesus the author and finisher of our faith: who for the joy that was set before him endured the cross, despising the shame" (Heb. 12:2).

Our Lord was able to endure the horrible death of the cross with all its physical, mental, and spiritual anguish because He knew what His sacrifice would do. It would save you, it would save me, and it would save all the people of the world who humbly submit their lives in obedience to Him. Bringing salvation into the world—that was His joy.

Love—how wonderful agape love is! When agape love is our motivation, no sacrifice is too great. Some people think because Jesus was not only human but also divine, all He went through during His short, precious time on this earth was easy for Him. They seem to take comfort in this, thinking, "surely, being only human, we are not expected to sacrifice our all." The Bible does not teach this line of thought.

When Jesus was in the garden on the Mount of Olives, He prayed, "Father, if thou be willing, remove this cup from me: nevertheless not my will, but thine, be done" (Luke 22:42). Why would Jesus pray to God and ask that He not have to go through the death of the cross, if it was His Father's will? After His prayer, the very next verse says,

"And there appeared an angel unto him from heaven, strengthening him" (v. 43). The human side of our Lord needed encouragement to endure the suffering of the cross. In verse 44 we read, "And being in an agony he prayed more earnestly: and his sweat was as it were great drops of blood falling down to the ground." I'm told "as it were great drops of sweat as blood" is not just a figure of speech; but this can happen under extremely stressful situations. Does this sound as if His sacrifice was easy because our Lord was not only human but divine? No, it was an agonizing sacrifice because he was not only divine but also human.

There are sacrifices on the mission field. For most of us women I believe the greatest sacrifices will be those involving our family, in one way or another. Let's face it, as strong as we want to be spiritually, we enjoy being around our precious family. When we are young missionaries going overseas, it means leaving our parents and our brothers and sisters. It means not seeing our children enjoying their grandparents. It means not seeing "Grandpa and Grandma" spending many hours with our children on their laps. It's having a child overseas and Mom is not there to share the joy with you. It's your children growing up in a crowded, polluted city, never knowing the beautiful, peaceful life of the country and the simple joys of God's creation. When the holidays come, oh how we miss the gathering of all our family together! When we grow older and our children one by one are ready for college, it means leaving them in the U.S. on their own and going to the other side of the world. When they marry and have children, it means being a "long-distance Grandma," not the kind you've always wanted to be. Hugs and kisses just aren't as good written on paper! We must leave our aged parents, not knowing if they will be on this earth on our next visit home.

Sometimes the physical hardships seem to be big sacrifices. Some countries are very hot and humid, and we Americans are accustomed to air conditioning in our cars, homes, stores, workplaces, and church buildings. Have you ever slept under wet sheets because the heat is so unbearable? When the weather turns cold, we turn on the heat very conveniently, but not so in all countries. Transportation can be very different, if you have transportation at all, other than your own two legs! Just buying groceries for the week can be a sacrifice to some women. Many women don't want to have to buy meats, fruits, and vegetables at an open market with the unsanitary conditions that exist. One bit of advice for those going to the open market: during the summer months get up early so you can beat the flies to the meat stands. Also make sure to choose your fruits and vegetables from the ones that are above ground level, where the stray dogs roaming the markets may have decided to relieve themselves. Sometimes it's not only the heat that makes the leafy vegetables look wilted!

On the mission field there is the sacrifice of Christian fellowship, especially the first few years when you haven't learned the language well enough to really have fellowship in the worship services and Bible studies. One really misses being among English-speaking brothers and sisters. Not being able to communicate well is very hard because it cuts you off from the new world in which you find yourself. The more quickly you can learn the language, the happier you'll be.

There are many other sacrifices and harder ones than those mentioned encountered on the mission field, but let us look at Hebrews 11:35-38 for a true insight into sacrifice and suffering.

> And others were tortured, not accepting deliverance; that they might obtain a better resurrection: and others had trial of cruel mockings and scourgings, yea, moreover of bonds and imprisonment; they were stoned, they were sawn asunder, were tempted, were slain with the sword: they wandered about in sheepskins and goatskins; being destitute, afflicted, tormented; (of whom the world was not worthy:) they wandered in deserts, and in mountains, and in dens and caves of the earth.

Even to these great sacrifices Paul says, "For I reckon that the sufferings of this present time are not worthy to be compared with the glory which shall be revealed in us" (Rom. 8:18).

When considering sacrifices to do missionary work, we aren't even considering torture, stoning, or other such persecution. It's the conveniences and the happy times with family and friends we don't want to sacrifice! Sisters, how can we learn to sacrifice to the degree God would have us to if we won't even give up our conveniences? We must think positively and count our blessings—and there are many on the mission field—and not our sacrifices.

People in countries other than ours have been brought up in cultures which may have many similarities with the American culture, or which may be totally different. America was founded on Christian principles and a faith in the God of the Bible. Nearly every American knows who Jesus is, and most people have a Bible in their home. Many countries are completely the opposite.

For instance, Asians believe in many gods. They believe their dead relatives become gods, so they also worship them. Their gods must constantly be appeased by animal and food sacrifices; otherwise, they believe they will do them and their family harm in some way. Many Asian people have a special room with an altar where they worship and sacrifice. On different days in the month, they set up tables in front of their homes. They fill the table with animal sacrifices, fruit and vegetable sacrifices, and drink offerings. I thought it rather amusing to see a large bottle of *Diet* Coke offered as a drink offering. I guess the gods have a weight problem too!

When a society has been built not upon Christian principles but upon heathen ones with all their superstitions, the people have a completely different outlook on life. They don't value life as the Christian does.

The missionary wife has to realize this and try to understand why they believe as they do. Then she can help to show them the truth without putting them down and making them feel that she thinks they are ignorant for holding to beliefs and traditions which are thousands of years old.

She has to understand how the society feels about family life. When a woman becomes a Christian, it may be very difficult for her to go back into her family as wife, daughter, and daughter-in-law. As the wife, she is responsible for the family's worship to idols. If the husband has not become a Christian, he may be very upset that she no longer wants to take part in idol worship.

One of our sisters in Taiwan had this very problem. Her husband beat her and twisted her legs so she could not walk to worship services. In all her mistreatment by him, she never said anything bad about him. She only said that she understood how he felt. He thought of Christianity as a Western religion. Since she had become a Christian, he felt he had lost his Chinese wife and felt embarrassment in his family when she no longer worshiped idols. She taught me a great lesson on understanding.

Two cultures may be very different, and neither may be wrong. In America it is very impolite for a man to belch at the table, much less a woman. In Asia, it is quite the contrary. I remember we had only been in Taiwan a couple of months. Our family had been invited for supper by a well-to-do Chinese Christian family on the most celebrated night of the year, Chinese New Year. We all put on our best clothes, and I reminded my children to be very polite. (No "Yuk! what's this?")

Our hostess, dressed very elegantly, met us at the door. We all sat down to a large feast. While we were eating, the cook kept bringing more delicious dishes. We were all getting very full. Our elegant hostess put her chopsticks down, relaxed a moment, and then let out a belch louder than any man's I've ever heard! I was in shock! Then, my children and I looked at each other, and we began to giggle and giggle, with our heads turned and napkins over our mouths trying not to be noticed. I finally had to leave the room to compose myself. She never said excuse me or looked the least bit embarrassed.

There was another missionary family dining with us that evening. They had been on the island a number of years. I later asked them about the incident, and they told me belching was not considered impolite, but a compliment to the cook.

The missionary wife needs to understand and appreciate the good things in the culture in which she is living. She must never try to make the people Americans, but only Christians of their own country.

Few will stay very long in a foreign country to preach the gospel without compassion for the masses of unbelievers. America looks like a ghost town compared to some countries. Asia is the most populated area of the world, yet so very, very few people have the opportunity to hear the pure gospel. We Americans must thank God every day for living in a country influenced by Christianity. In other countries it is so different.

Something I will never get use to seeing is handicapped people, crawling on the filthy, muddy market floors, begging for money or selling some small object. They literally crawl or slide, pushing a little wagon in front of them. Their poor bodies are so badly twisted. All I can think is, "How could a parent let his child do such a degrading and painful thing?" Does your heart not fill with compassion for people like this—not only for the handicapped child, but the parents also? For you see, they have not grown up knowing the love of God as we have. Life itself is not precious in their eyes. In the summer, the streets get hot, yet beggars are still there, sliding along the market streets.

I asked a sister about this situation. She told me there are those who make a business of the handicapped people. Parents may sell their handicapped child to someone who has a number of handicapped people. The owner will give them a place to sleep and food to eat in return for begging money for them. The handicapped person never gets any of the money, only room and board. He is trapped because of his condition.

There are no laws in Taiwan to forbid begging that might put a stop to this inhumane business. A number of years ago, children were stolen, a hand or leg was cut off them, and they were placed somewhere to beg.

Where God is not in the hearts of people, any evil is possible and very probable. Is it no wonder why God has commanded Christians to go into all the world to preach the gospel? Only the gospel can clean and purify an evil mind.

Jesus was full of compassion, both for the physical problems of people and for the spiritual need of their souls.

> But when he saw the multitudes, he was moved with compassion on them, because they fainted, and were scattered abroad, as sheep having no shepherd. Then saith he unto his disciples, The harvest truly is plenteous, but the labourers are few; pray ye therefore the Lord of the harvest, that he will send forth labourers into his harvest (Matt. 9:36-38)

There are so many people in this world who are ignorant of the saving message. Their souls will be damned to hell if they never have the opportunity to hear the good news. How can we who know the truth ever think it too great a sacrifice to leave our country for a portion of our lives to help someone else know the saving message? Yes, the missionary wife must be full of compassion for the lost.

Seeing the masses of people on the streets and idols everywhere sometimes can be overwhelming. One wonders, "How can we possibly make a difference?" This is where being optimistic is of great worth. We've all heard about the two shoe salesmen who traveled to Africa. One salesman phoned back and said, "There is no business here— they don't wear shoes." The other salesman said, "Send me all the shoes you can—no one has shoes!" So it is in the countries with so many people. Yes, there are lots of people, but that only means there will be more of the few that will gladly receive the word. The missionary's work is to preach the gospel and let the power of the gospel change people's lives. Surely, if it was only of ourselves, we never could make a difference in anyone's life.

The optimistic missionary wife will look at living in a different culture as a blessing for her whole family. She will realize the great benefit of her children growing up with the native children, learning to speak their language, and becoming their friends. Her children will learn to love all the different faces of the world. They will learn how difficult and sometimes lonely it is to be foreigners. It will make them appreciate foreigners in their own country, and they will want to be kind and helpful. They will not think of foreigners as ignorant because they speak English with an accent. Optimism turns all that's negative into positive, and the missionary wife and her family will adjust to the new culture more quickly with an optimistic attitude.

When leaving familiar surroundings and making a new home in a new land, an adventurous spirit and a sense of humor go a long way. Everything is different, from the way the people look and act, to the new language, to all the new customs, to the different way you have to go about doing everyday chores, to the food, and even to the odors in the air!

One of the first things to be done is to find a place to live and buy the necessary furnishings. The missionaries who had been on the island for a number of years were very kind in helping us with this, but one day Joe and I set out on our own. There we were in a big crowded foreign city, not knowing how to say anything in Chinese but "thank you."

We went from store to store looking at furniture. When we found something we liked, my husband would say *"Ra cha chyan,"* and the salesman would write how much on a piece of paper. I asked him what he was saying. He said he'd heard others say it and figured it must be, "How much money is it?" Whatever he was saying, it was working, and we felt good that we were able to get around on our own.

A few weeks later, when we started language school, one of the first phrases we learned was, "How much money?" Instead of *"Ra cha chyan,"* Joe should have been saying, *"Dwo shau chyan."* I guess he got the last word right, *chyan,* which means "money," and they knew what the old foreigner meant. We had a good laugh, and to this day, I still tease him about it every once in a while.

Learning a new language can be quite a chore and very depressing if it is not done with fun. Learning to communicate in a foreign language is an adventure in itself. There are the many drills in the classroom, saying the basic words with the different tones. You must say them over and over, getting the tones just right, until you feel your tongue is wrapped around your head several times. Then the big step—taking what you've learned that week onto the streets to try to communicate with the native people. I remember, time and time again, thinking I knew exactly how to say what I wanted. But, no matter how hard I tried, using all the different tones, hoping I would say it right at least once, the salesman wouldn't understand until I began playing charades. It seemed my acting was better than my Chinese! After using my hands, and whatever else I thought would help, they would understand and go running to get what I wanted. Needless to say, shopping took me much longer in those days, but each time was a good laugh!

The missionary wife cannot be fearful. She must cast out fear and replace it with boldness. She must be like Peter and John and pray, "Grant unto thy servants, that with all boldness they may speak thy word" (Acts 4:29).

Doing the Lord's work, such as passing out tracts to people, teaching ladies' classes, leading women in prayer, or conducting one-on-one Bible studies can be fearful for some. Many missionary wives have to do this using another language, and this can compound the fear, so they refrain from trying.

The missionary wife has left home and family for the sole purpose of teaching lost souls the gospel of Christ. She cannot let fear of any kind get in the way of her purpose for being on the mission field. She cannot be satisfied with thinking that, as long as she takes care of the home, she has done her part. True, this is very important; it enables her husband to be free to preach the gospel. She must be bold and believe the Lord's promise, "I can do all things through Christ which strengtheneth me" (Phil. 4:13). With preparation and making oneself take the gospel to others, boldness and confidence will fill her heart where once there was only fear.

She must have a bold and confident spirit, for she will not always be working with her husband. Many times she will be working with a new convert who depends on her for strength to go door knocking or to teach a friend the gospel. Where there is fear, there is no progress. The missionary wife must be bold as the first century Christians who, in spite of trials and persecutions, dared to teach lost souls the saving gospel.

One takes on a lot of responsibility when she becomes a missionary wife. On the mission field, much of the time, the missionary's wife and her family are the only congregation of the Lord's people for many miles around. The growth of the church depends on them. Since the missionary wife is the only Christian woman in the congregation, for a while all the Christian woman's responsibilities fall on her. She must keep the church building clean, make the unleavened bread, and sometimes squeeze the grapes for grape juice when it's not available. She must make sure the communion table is prepared on Sunday. She picks up neighborhood children for Bible class. She is the children's Bible class teacher, the nursery attendant, and the ladies' Bible class teacher. She is in charge of organizing and mak-

ing most of the food for get-togethers. She also has responsibilities in any benevolent work. She is church secretary
and much more.

I believe her biggest responsibility is teaching the Christian women to take on these responsibilities, so they will
grow spiritually and, very importantly, so the church will
be able to carry on as a faithful congregation when the
missionaries go back home.

The missionary wife must remember that just as a
mother is to train up her children in the ways of the Lord
so one day they can function as faithful Christian adults,
so she has the responsibility, to the best of her ability, to
train her sisters in Christ to be capable, active members in
the church.

I can't imagine being a preacher's wife, much less a
missionary's wife, without a love for teaching God's Word.
I believe women are blessed with the most enjoyable role
in teaching—we teach the children! Their pure hearts are
open to what we teach them. The lessons they learn and
the way they are taught to see God will remain with them
for the rest of their lives. Unless there is another missionary's wife working with her, this great responsibility falls
solely on the one person until others are converted and
taught to be teachers.

In many countries on the mission field, teaching materials cannot be found, so the missionary's wife must bring
from the U.S. what is suitable for where she is teaching.
She has to make many of the visuals using the language of
the country. Hopefully assisted by a native of the country,
she must translate all children's Bible class songs so they
may be used in Bible class. She also has to make up all her
own lessons using the native language. This takes much
more time because almost everything must be done from
scratch. If she doesn't enjoy teaching and does not realize
the important role she has in molding each child's soul,
she will not put the time and effort necessary into this
great service which is her privilege as the missionary's wife.

I remember my first children's Bible class on Sunday morning in the city of Hualien. We had painted the classroom, and I put visuals up and prepared my lesson with the help of my Chinese teacher. I was very nervous because I would have to teach and sing in Chinese. I had put lots of time into it, so I was hoping to have more than just a couple of children come besides my own preschooler and toddler boys. To my surprise, I had more children than chairs—eighteen children attended that first class! They aged from my toddler to eight years old. I was blessed to teach many of those children every Sunday for several years until we left there and moved to the city of Taichung to start a congregation.

As the missionary family begins to establish the Lord's church in a foreign country, they are the representatives of God. By their Christian example the native people learn much about the true God of heaven.

In many countries we Americans, with our fair skin and hair, stick out like a sore thumb. We are watched constantly whenever we step outside our doors. The neighbors will stand outside the gate just to watch you and your children playing in the yard. I remember when we first moved to Taiwan we took our children to the park. To our surprise, small crowds of people began following our family. If we stopped, they stopped. If we moved on, they followed. They enjoyed very much watching us play ball with our children and would cheer as one of the children caught it. When going to the market to buy vegetables, all eyes are on the missionary's wife. What's really interesting is when you begin to understand the language and you hear what they are saying about you. They are not expecting the foreigner to understand. They stand in amazement when you turn to reply to them in their native tongue, and then we all have a good laugh.

All the attention can get bothersome after a while, but it's very important to be kind and cheerful to them. When my children get tired of all the attention, I say, "Be thankful they like us and are not throwing stones at us."

As the unbelievers become Christians, they look to the missionary family as examples for them. They see the love of God by the way we treat each other. They learn how to be a Christian wife and mother by how the missionary wife conducts herself, not only during services, but when she invites members into their home. They look to her as their example of modest dress and how to dress for worship services. Their eyes are upon us. Our lights must shine and we must live what we preach before them.

Being hospitable is important wherever one lives, but especially so in a country where in many homes there is little warmth. The missionary's wife can use her home as a great tool for the kingdom. A neat homey atmosphere makes people comfortable and relaxed. Add to this love and laughter, and you have what many people are looking for. They begin to see that the Christian family is different from theirs, and they want to learn more so they can have the same happiness. Many times I've heard comments from believers and unbelievers alike about how happy Christians are. The wise missionary's wife will open her home with love to all her sisters and brothers to help make them feel they are one family of God. This is especially important to those who don't have a warm family life. It will help to keep them faithful to God.

Only with our relationships in the right order, with God as our first love, can we love our husbands with all our heart. The missionary's wife has to love her husband enough to let him be free to preach the gospel wherever he has the opportunity. Her love must be strong enough to be willing to spend a good part of her time apart from him without being bitter, but finding joy in seeing her husband using his talents to his fullest potential for the cause of Christ.

The missionaries many times go into a city and start a congregation of the Lord's people from scratch. There are no brothers in Christ to help the missionary husband, so he must make all the visits and conduct all the Bible studies. This takes much of his time day and night.

Also, as the missionary family works in a foreign country, many times the missionary husband begins to reach out into other countries in that part of the world. This means a couple may be separated for weeks or months at a time. I'm not advocating the husband neglect his God-given responsibilities as husband and father. The two must discuss the family's needs and decide accordingly how often he can be away from the family.

I believe as the missionary's wife loves God with all her heart she will have the love for her husband that will help him to do all that God would have him to do in His kingdom. Together, as a team, working in the greatest cause on this earth, they will find great joy and add richness to their marriage and secure for themselves an eternity in Heaven.

There are many other qualities of a missionary's wife we could study, but of those we have discussed, do you see any qualities that God has required only of her? Does God not expect all Christian women to have these same qualities, whether Bible class teacher, elder's or deacon's wife, Christian mother or wife, preacher's wife, young Christian, or older Christian? When each Christian woman loves God with all her heart, and with all her soul, and with all her mind, she will develop these qualities. The only difference in a missionary's wife is that she truly tries to go where God, through His providence, leads her, rather than just singing, "Lord Send Me."

Note of Gratitude:

Much appreciation to Janis Dearman, my fellow missionary's wife and "Grandma" to our precious granddaughters for her encouraging words and editing my unskilled writing.

13

For Church Leaders' Wives
Debbie Kea

In my judgment one of the greatest needs in the church today is leadership. The church cries out for dedicated men who will sacrifice to guide God's people in paths of righteousness.

Support

One of the reasons I believe we do not have enough men to step up and fill the need is we do not have enough women willing to help them. We have too many selfish women who hinder their husbands from growing and serving and using their talents. There is no doubt that a woman's attitude can make or break her husband when it comes to his effectiveness. I know a woman whose husband was being considered to be an elder. When I asked her how she felt about it, she frowned severely and moaned, "I begged him not to do this!" This same woman today wonders why her husband wasn't effective. How could he be when she didn't encourage, help, or admire him?

Admiration is a must, women. There's not a man alive who doesn't have an ego. Men need to be admired. This helps their confidence, and they must have confidence if they are to be leaders. I recall a young woman who complained to me about her husband deciding to preach. She came to the wrong person for sympathy. I told her to repent. What greater thing could she want him to do? He was proclaiming God's Word and saving eternal souls. She should be so proud of him. I think deep down her anguish was not so much over his being a preacher but her being a preacher's wife. She believed being a preacher's wife would require more of her than she was willing to give. I reminded her that preachers' wives are required by God to be the same as any Christian woman—faithful.

Every husband needs support, but elders, deacons, and preachers need a special kind. They endure pressures, criticisms, and betrayals. These things happen in the world, of course, but when they happen in the church, when it's your own brethren who are supposed to love you, they are even more devastating. Wives provide the constant, unwavering support a man needs to carry on.

Submission

The wives of church leaders are to be in submission to their own husbands as all wives are (Eph. 5:22-25). Being married to an elder or a preacher gives you no authority. This is a *vital* lesson. My husband instructed me long ago that when I am questioned by brethren I am to answer one thing: "Go talk to the elders." And it works every time. I remember a good sister specifically who was scolding me about what she thought my husband the preacher should be doing. She expected me to make some changes; after all, I must have influence! I directed her to my husband's office and told her to take it up with him. She never pressured me again. I know another elder's wife who sat next to the doorway so she could hear the elders' meeting. She would then give her two-cents'-worth to her husband later. This was not her job. Naturally, quite often wives do know what's the elders' or preacher's business. We must be very careful not to reveal these things, and we must be ready to discourage the questions of the curious.

The part we play as elders' wives, deacons' wives, or preachers' wives is so important, but we must remember *we* are not the elders, deacons, or preachers. Our opinions and advice are valuable to our husbands, but they only count when they're asked for!

We cannot forget that Christ is the head of His kingdom, our husband is the head of our home, and we, as women, must willingly submit to their authority—even when our husbands are leaders.

Silence and Self-Control

Every leader's wife I've ever talked to has emphasized how important silence and self-control are in the life of a church leader's wife. It is just an absolute must. Of course self-control is so much a part of every Christian's life. Paul knew its value. He knew he could not be effective as a preacher if he didn't have self-control (1 Cor. 9:27). As a schoolteacher, I tell my high school students all the time, "You want to rule the world, but you can't control your own selves." The Proverbs writer said it best: "He that hath no rule over his own spirit is like a city that is broken down, and without walls" (Prov. 25:28); "He that is slow to anger is better than the mighty; and he that ruleth his spirit than he that taketh a city" (Prov. 16:32). As one elder's wife put it, self-control can "mean the difference between success and failure in most situations." In 1 Corinthians 13:5 love is described as "not easily provoked." If we are to show our love for God and man, and if we are to be the wives who are truly suitable helpers, we must endeavor to have self-control and know when silence truly is golden.

Struggles

There are particular struggles common only to church leaders' wives. I can't cover them all, but I will cover those I think occur most often.

Elders' wives:

1. Wives of newly appointed elders may experience a change in the way some people treat them. Some may

distance themselves from you, whereas before they were very friendly.

2. Another difficulty some elders' wives have is seeing their husbands working out serious problems in the church, seeing the long hours they put in, without receiving any consideration from the church family.

3. Always one of the biggest struggles is trying to get more people involved in the work of the church, relieving some of the work on your husband, but most important, fulfilling their obligation to God.

Preachers' Wives:

1. Like elders' wives, preachers' wives are often treated differently. Sometimes perfection is expected; after all, you are married to a man of God. Seldom are you considered friend material because most preachers' wives are thought to be unapproachable. We have to make an extra effort to let our brethren know that we are as human as anyone, that we love deeply and hurt the same way.

2. Most preachers' wives struggle with the Wonder Woman Syndrome at some time or other. You know the one—where you have to be the best wife, mother, personal worker, and entertainer. I think every preacher's wife has to come to terms with the fact that you can't do everything. You try, and you beat yourself up when you can't do it all. Finally you discover God expects you to do your best at only what you can do.

3. Your first struggle may be with your husband when you find out he's not perfect. He preaches a perfect message but he is a man who must grow. Let me ask you—you know the Scripture, so why aren't you perfect? Everybody falls short and must have time to grow.

4. You may struggle to raise your children in the nurture and admonition of the Lord. They are under a microscope most of their lives and that can be a difficult thing. I have always made it clear to my children that if their father were a carpenter, we would still do the things we do because we are Christians, not because Dad is a preacher. I think that attitude changes their outlook on the whole Christian life. Of course, the best way to overcome trouble with your kids is to live the right life before them. They will nearly always model you.

5. For many who are preachers' wives, living in their husband's shadow proves to be a big struggle. If you are insecure, if you do not have a handle on your own identity, you will have trouble with this. Your husband is in the limelight; he will get a great deal of attention. Accept it; deal with it. That is the way your life will be. You must be big enough to be your own person, make your own friends, and have your own interests and conversations. If you don't, you will be very unhappy as a preacher's wife. If it bothers you that some don't know your name and always call you "the preacher's wife," if you wait to hear your husband mention you from the pulpit, if you get mad when your opinion is not sought, just his, if when people walk past you and shake his hand, you feel hurt or offended, *get over yourself!* It's going to happen. Lighten up, be your own person, get out there and shake hands yourself, let the brethren know you love them, and you'll stop noticing it before long.

Deacons' wives:

1. Again, you may be treated differently once your husband becomes a deacon.

2. You may become accustomed to your husband's time often being taken up with church work. You may find

yourself resenting the time he is gone. Don't give in to this response. Talk to him about needing to make a special time to be with you, let him know you miss him, but don't make him ever feel guilty for what he does for the Lord. This is a problem for all church leaders.

3. A deacon's wife whom I consider one of the finest Christians I've ever known gave me this advice: "Smile and be friendly, be hospitable, treat all people as being special; be no respecter of persons, study God's Word daily, and use the King James Bible for study purposes." I can't improve upon that!

Scriptures to Help

Though you may receive help and invaluable guidance from women whose husbands are leaders, your true aid that will never fail you comes only from the Lord and His Word. Below I have listed some specific Scriptures that women have mentioned to me as being a help or comfort to them in their lives as wives of church leaders. I have also included some of my own.

1. Philippians 4:13—"I can do all things through Christ which strengtheneth me." These are truly words of encouragement to all of us. When we feel downtrodden or maybe even a bit of a failure, this verse should serve to boost us back up.

2. 1 Peter 2:21—"Christ also suffered for us, leaving us an example, that ye should follow his steps." Whatever happens, we must never take our eyes off of our Lord, ever striving to be like Him.

3. 1 Peter 3:8-12—"Finally, be ye all of one mind, having compassion one of another, love as brethren, be pitiful, be courteous: not rendering evil for evil, or railing

for railing: but contrariwise blessing; knowing that ye are thereunto called, that ye should inherit a blessing. For he that will love life, and see good days, let him refrain his tongue from evil, and his lips that they speak no guile: let him eschew evil, and do good; let him seek peace, and ensue it. For the eyes of the Lord are over the righteous, and his ears are open unto their prayers: but the face of the Lord is against them that do evil."

These words are so fitting to provide us with the guidance for treating our brethren as Christians should. The petty jealousies, the selfishness, the hurt feelings, the vengeful acts—all these will disappear at the living out of these verses.

4. 1 Thessalonians 5:16—"Rejoice evermore." Find joy in your work for the Lord.

5. 2 Thessalonians 2:13-14—"But we are bound to give thanks alway to God for you, brethren beloved of the Lord, because God hath from the beginning chosen you to salvation through sanctification of the Spirit and belief of the truth; whereunto he called you by our gospel, to the obtaining of the glory of our Lord Jesus Christ." Don't forget to pray for your brethren always as Paul did. And be so thankful for all the prayers offered on your behalf. No one will ever know how much it means to me every time I hear my name and the names of my husband and family brought to God in prayer at worship. It humbles you; it changes you.

6. Proverbs 31:11-12—"The heart of her husband doth safely trust in her, so that he shall have no need of spoil. She will do him good and not evil all the days of her life." Live so your husband will safely trust in you. Make it your mission to do him good all the days of your life.

7. 1 Timothy 2:9-10—"In like manner also, that women adorn themselves in modest apparel, with shamefacedness and sobriety; not with broided hair, or gold, or pearls, or costly array; but (which becometh women professing godliness) with good works." It is very important to dress appropriately at all church functions, and don't forget to dress modestly at home as well. You never know when someone is going to drop by.

8. Ephesians 5:22-33—"Wives, submit yourselves unto your own husbands, as unto the Lord. For the husband is the head of the wife, even as Christ is the head of the church: and he is the saviour of the body. Therefore as the church is subject unto Christ, so let the wives be to their own husbands in every thing. Husbands, love your wives, even as Christ also loved the church, and gave himself for it . . . Nevertheless let every one of you in particular so love his wife even as himself; and the wife see that she reverence her husband." This is God's plan, and when it is followed, we will understand a great measure of happiness. I have always believed that if men love us like Christ loved the church—and that's an awful lot of love!—we will have no trouble submitting ourselves to them.

Finally

The church is in dire need of great leaders. Thus, the church is in dire need of great leaders' wives. May it be our prayer that God will raise up women to be the suitable helpers for these men, that those of us who are in these positions will mold our lives into God's vessels, and those who are soon to be in the position of a leader's wife will determine to grow in the grace and knowledge of our Lord for the benefit of themselves, their husbands, and the church.